Microsoft®
Access 2010:
Level 1 of 3

PAMELA R. TOLIVER
Soft-Spec, LLC

LABYRINTH
LEARNING™

El Sobrante, CA

Microsoft Access 2010: Level 1
by Pamela R. Toliver

Copyright © 2011 by Labyrinth Learning

Labyrinth Learning
P.O. Box 20818
El Sobrante, California 24820
800.522.9746
On the web at lablearning.com

President:
Brian Favro

Product Development Manager:
Jason Favro

Managing Editor:
Laura A. Lionello

Production Manager:
Rad Proctor

eLearning Production Manager:
Arl S. Nadel

Editorial/Production Team:
Donna Bacidore, Pamela Beveridge,
Belinda Breyer, Everett Cowan, Alec Fehl,
Alona Harris, Sandy Jones, PMG Media

Indexing: Joanne Sprott

Interior Design:
Mark Ong, Side-by-Side Studios

Cover Design:
Words At Work

ITEM: 1-59136-317-9
ISBN-13: 978-1-59136-317-0

Manufactured in the United States of America.

10 9 8 7 6 5 4 3 2

Table of Contents

Quick Reference Tables   v
Preface   vi

LESSON 1: EXPLORING ACCESS 2010   2

Defining Access Databases   4
  What Is a Database?   4
  Identifying Database Structures   4
  Organizing Data into Database Tables   5
  Storing Your Exercise Files   6
Exploring the Access Environment   7
  Launching Access 2010   7
Identifying Elements of the Access Window   9
  Creating a Blank Database   9
Identifying Features of the Database Window   12
  Using the Navigation Pane   12
Creating Tables in Datasheet View   15
  Working with Tables   15
  Identifying Table Guidelines   16
  Identifying Reserved Words   17
  Requiring Data in Key Fields   17
  Identifying Field Data Types   17
  Navigating Tables and Entering Data   19
  Using AutoCorrect   20
  Working with Tabs and Closing
   Database Objects   20
Previewing and Printing Data   22
  Setting Up Data to Print   22
  Examining the Preview Window   22
Using Help   25
  Access Help and Databases   25
Closing a Database and Exiting Access   27
Concepts Review   27
Reinforce Your Skills   28
Apply Your Skills   30
Critical Thinking & Work-Readiness Skills   31

LESSON 2: BUILDING A DATABASE   32

Designing a Database   34
  Planning a Database Design   34
  Documenting a Database Design   34
Opening a Database   35
  Enabling Macros Controlling
   Database Security   35
Saving a Database as a New File   38
  Using the Save As Command   38
Opening Database Objects   39
  Identifying Database Objects   39
  Opening Existing Database Objects   41
  Navigating Records in a Table Datasheet   42
Creating Database Objects   43
  Creating and Using Forms   43
  Entering Data Using Datasheets and Forms   45
  Creating and Generating Reports   47
Creating Tables Using Other Techniques   50
  Displaying and Using Table Design View   50
  Creating a Table from an Excel Worksheet   54
Creating a New Database Using a Template   57
Managing Databases and Database Objects   59
  Saving Database Objects as New Objects   59
  Backing Up a Database   61
Concepts Review   62
Reinforce Your Skills   63
Apply Your Skills   66
Critical Thinking & Work-Readiness Skills   69

LESSON 3: MAINTAINING A DATABASE 70

LESSON 4: QUERYING A DATABASE 122

Formatting a Table Datasheet Layout	72
Changing the Width of Columns	72
Moving and Hiding Data Columns	72
Saving a Table Layout	73
Enhancing a Datasheet	75
Modifying Table Structures	78
Renaming Tables and Editing, Adding, and Deleting Table Fields	78
Setting Lookup Fields Using the Lookup Wizard	81
Examining the Benefits of Lookup Tables	82
Performing a Lookup	82
Setting Field Properties	85
Why Set Field Properties?	86
Setting Field Size	86
Setting Captions	86
Formatting Data Using Input Masks	86
Setting Validation Rules	92
Setting Default Field Values	94
Retrieving Data	95
Sorting Records	95
Sorting Records Using Multiple Fields	97
Locating and Deleting Records Using Table Datasheets	99
Using Forms to Locate and Edit Records	102
Using Find and Replace to Update Records	102
Filtering Records	103
Filtering Records by Form	105
Previewing and Printing Data	108
Setting Up Data to Print	108
Concepts Review	108
Reinforce Your Skills	109
Apply Your Skills	115
Critical Thinking & Work-Readiness Skills	120

Creating Select Queries	124
Reviewing Query Features	124
Identifying Tools for Creating Select Queries	124
Creating a Select Query Using Query Design	127
Designing a Query Using Multiple Tables	132
Choosing Fields to Include in a Query	132
Selecting a Field Appearing in Multiple Tables	132
Setting Query Criteria	134
Adding Criteria to a Query	134
Using Wildcards	136
Setting AND and OR Criteria	137
Entering Date Criteria	140
Sorting a Query and Limiting Results	141
Setting a Query Sort Order	141
Limiting Number of Results Displayed	141
Performing Calculations in Queries	143
Identifying Parts of a Calculated Field	144
Creating and Formatting a Calculated Field	145
Using a Function in a Query Expression	146
Creating Special Types of Queries	151
Creating a Crosstab Query	151
Creating Unmatched and Duplicates Queries	154
Viewing Structured Query Language (SQL)	156
Concepts Review	157
Reinforce Your Skills	158
Apply Your Skills	164
Critical Thinking & Work-Readiness Skills	169
Index	170

Quick Reference Tables

DATABASE TASKS

Backing Up and Repairing Databases 61
Copying Database Objects 60
Creating a Database Using a Template 57
Creating Database Objects 43
Identifying Common Field Properties 85
Identifying Object Types in Access Databases 41
Importing Excel Data to Create a Table 55
Setting Value Validation Comparisons 93

GENERAL TASKS

Copying Database Objects 60
Defining Comparison Indicators and Symbols 106
Defining Wildcard Symbols 136
Formatting Data Using Input Mask Symbols 87
Identifying the Order of Mathematical Calculations 145
Using Find and Replace 100

QUERY TASKS

Creating Crosstab, Unmatched, and Duplicates Queries Using Wizards 152
Identifying the Order of Mathematical Calculations 145
Setting a Query Sort Order 142
Using AND and OR Criteria 137
Using Calculated Dates in Expressions 145
Using Query Design 129

RECORD TASKS

Adding a New Record to a Table 46
Deleting Records 99
Sorting Records 98

TABLE TASKS

Formatting Data Using Input Mask Symbols 87
Identifying Access Data Types 51
Sorting Records 98
Using Find and Replace 100

Preface

Microsoft® Access 2010: Level 1 provides thorough training of Access 2010 introductory skills. This course is supported with comprehensive instructor resources and our eLab assessment and learning management tool. And, our new work-readiness exercises ensure students have the critical thinking skills necessary to succeed in today's world. After completing this course, students will be able to successfully face the challenges presented in the next book in this series, *Microsoft Access 2010: Level 2*.

Visual Conventions

This book uses many visual and typographic cues to guide students through the lessons. This page provides examples and describes the function of each cue.

Type this text	Anything you should type at the keyboard is printed in this typeface.
	Tips, Notes, and Warnings are used throughout the text to draw attention to certain topics.
Command→ Command→ Command, etc.	This convention indicates how to give a command from the Ribbon. The commands are written: Ribbon Tab→Command Group→Command→ Subcommand.
FROM THE KEYBOARD [Ctrl]+[S] to save	These margin notes indicate shortcut keys for executing a task described in the text.

Exercise Progression

The exercises in this book build in complexity as students work through a lesson toward mastery of the skills taught.

■ **Develop Your Skills** exercises are introduced immediately after concept discussions. They provide detailed, step-by-step tutorials.

■ **Reinforce Your Skills** exercises provide additional hands-on practice with moderate assistance.

■ **Apply Your Skills** exercises test students' skills by describing the correct results without providing specific instructions on how to achieve them.

■ **Critical Thinking and Work-Readiness Skills** exercises are the most challenging. They provide generic instructions, allowing students to use their skills and creativity to achieve the results they envision.

Exploring Access 2010

LESSON OUTLINE

1.1   Defining Access Databases
1.2   Exploring the Access Environment
1.3   Identifying Elements of the Access Window
1.4   Identifying Features of the Database Window
1.5   Creating Tables in Datasheet View
1.6   Previewing and Printing Data
1.7   Using Help
1.8   Closing a Database and Exiting Access
1.9   Concepts Review
Reinforce Your Skills
Apply Your Skills
Critical Thinking & Work-Readiness Skills

LEARNING OBJECTIVES

After studying this lesson, you will be able to:

- Define database and key terms associated with databases
- Identify objects contained in modern databases and explain how they are used
- Launch Access 2010 and identify elements of the application window
- Create a new blank database and database table
- Use the Navigation Pane and enter data into a table
- Save and close database objects
- Preview and print datasheets
- Use Help
- Close a database and exit Access 2010

Have you ever wondered how service agents who take your order over the telephone know what questions to ask about the products you order...or how sportscasters come up with little-known facts about teams and players in a flash? In most cases, these service agents and sportscasters have access to a powerful database from which they obtain the information.

In this lesson, you will explore elements of the Microsoft Access 2010 application window, create a new database, and identify features of the database window. As you explore the tools available in Access 2010, you will begin building the new database.

Student Resources   labyrinthelab.com/acc10

Updating Raritan Clinic East

Raritan Clinic East is an incorporated medical practice staffed by the finest clinical diagnosticians in the Pediatric fields of General Medicine, Cardiology, Orthopedics, Pediatric, Emergency Medicine, and Neonatology. The practice serves a patient community ranging in ages from newborn to 18 years.

Raritan Clinic East

Pediatric Diagnostic Specialists

Recently, Raritan Clinic East has moved to a new facility located on a wooded six-acre site in the center of Raritan's vast medical professional complex. The 21,000-square-foot state-of-the-art facility was completed in 2009.

James Elliott has recently accepted a position in the human resources department with Raritan Clinic East. He has been tasked with reviewing the current records management system. From this review, he will be able to determine how best to organize data in new databases created using Access 2010. Then he will create a new database in which to store the data so that information can be located and retrieved more efficiently.

The first thing James notices is that the data laid out in the current database contains too many details in each column and the database has data for multiple employee groups all together in one large file.

ID	Name	Address	Date Hired	Telephone	DOB
1	Kayla Walker, M.D.	234 Hanson Dr., San Diego, CA 92126	4/14/2006	(714) 555-8934	3/22/1974
2	Zachary Scott, M.D.	49 Racine, San Diego, CA 92118	8/30/2006	(612) 555-7575	8/2/1945
3	Jose Green, M.D.	55 Raine Rd., San Diego, CA 92126	9/1/2006	(609) 555-9000	3/26/1980
4	Julia Adams, R.N.	303 Ray Rd., San Diego, CA 92118	9/11/2006	(915) 555-7936	1/16/1949
5	Destiny Baker, R.N.	19 Cedar Grove Ct., San Diego, CA 92126	9/12/2006	(918) 555-8962	5/10/1987
6	Morgan Gonzalez	78 Cedar St., San Diego, CA 92118	9/12/2006	(713) 555-0711	8/18/1992
7	Kaitlyn Nelson	89 Cederwood Dr., San Diego, CA 92126	9/15/2006	(918) 555 8617	1/3/1952
8	Savannah Carter, R.N	39 Century Court, San Diego, CA 92118	9/15/2006	(603) 555-1000	12/12/1959
9	Katherine Mitchell	8900 Chadwicke Court, San Diego, CA 921	9/20/2006	(804) 555-5400	4/19/1969
10	Caleb Perez	754 Greves Court, San Diego, CA 92118	9/21/2006	(216) 555-4141	4/1/1976

The new database will have each detail separated from others.

Doctors

DoctorID	DrFirstName	DrLasstName	DrStreet	DrCity	DrState	DrZIP	DrDateHired	DrTelephone	DrDOB
1	Kayla	Walker	234 Hanson Dr.	San Diego	CA	92126	4/14/2006	(714) 555-8934	3/22/1974
2	Zachary	Scott	49 Racine	San Diego	CA	92118	8/30/2006	(612) 555-7575	8/2/1945
3	Jose	Green	55 Raine Rd	San Diego	CA	92126	9/1/2006	(609) 555-9000	3/26/1980

Nurses

NursesID	NrFirstName	NrLasstName	NrStreet	NrCity	NrState	NrZIP	NrDateHired	NrTelephone
1	Julia	Adams	303 Ray Rd.	Houston	TX	77002	9/11/2006	(915) 555-7936
2	Destiny	Baker	19 Cedar Grove Ct.	Tulsa	OK	74133	9/12/2006	(918) 555-8962

Related data—doctors and nurses—will be stored in separate tables.

1.1 Defining Access Databases

Video Lesson   labyrinthelab.com/videos

If you have ever used a phone book or a catalog, retrieved a note card from a card file, or pulled a file from a file cabinet, you have used a database. If you have ever used an index or a table of contents in a book, you have also used a database—just a different type of database. Each of these items consists of individual pieces of *data* that, when combined, make up a *database*.

What Is a Database?

A *database* is a collection of related data stored together in one electronic file. Historically, individuals and businesses have used databases to store vast amounts of data in an organized fashion to facilitate quick and easy retrieval of facts, figures, and information. Prior to the computer age, database records were stored on index cards, on columnar tablets, and in file folders stored in file cabinets. While these data storage methods are still around today, computer-based databases have reduced the storage requirements of data and have improved the efficiency of data retrieval. As a result, reports from sportscasters, historians, politicians, stock sales, unemployment records, and many other details can be reported with amazing accuracy—and very quickly.

Identifying Database Structures

Early electronic databases stored data in flat files—that is, in one gigantic pool of data all stored together like family photos stored in a large box. Flat files contained repetitive data in many entries.

Someone had to type this patient information four times and more, depending on the number of supplies used, room charges, etc.

Matthew	Spear	2122 Londin Ln	San Diego	CA	56119	6515554683	12/14/2010	X-Rays	12/14/2010
Melissa	Klein	291 South J St.	San Bernardino	CA	92444	9095554613	12/26/2010	Tonsillectomy	12/27/2010
Mia	Zamora	3453 Lakeside	San Diego	CA	48322	8985557587	9/3/2010	CBC	9/3/2010
Michael	Francis	1115 S. 11th Stre	Shawnee	CA	92190	6195552784	10/1/2010	Blood Work	10/3/2010
Michael	Francis	1115 S. 11th Stre	Shawnee	CA	92190	6195552784	10/1/2010	Appendectomy	10/3/2010
Michael	Francis	1115 S. 11th Stre	Shawnee	CA	92190	6195552784	10/1/2010	PostOp	10/3/2010
Michael	Francis	1115 S. 11th Stre	Shawnee	CA	92190	6195552784	10/1/2010	X-Rays	10/3/2010
Michael	Little	14 Sunset Blvd.	Towaoc	CO	81334	3035559669	3/13/2010	Observation	3/15/2010

Data entry in a flat file database requires lots of repetition.

Modern database programs, such as Access 2010, store data efficiently. Such database programs are often referred to as *relational databases* because they store related data in various tables to eliminate the need for repetitive data entry. For example, a clinic might place basic information about its patients—name, address, city, state, and ZIP—into one table, and data such as charges details—date of admission, item used, item description, number used, and unit price—into another table. A clinic might also place a list of doctors and data related to the doctors into one table and reference the doctor who worked with a patient to report patient charges. As a result, data processing becomes more efficient—data entry personnel can enter only data that is unique into the appropriate table rather than retyping data that is already stored in a different table.

Patient details are found in the Patients table.

Patient name is referenced in the Admissions table.

Doctor details appear in the Doctors table.

The doctor name is referenced as the admitting doctor in the Admissions table.

Organizing Data into Database Tables

It takes careful planning to organize database data into logical tables *before* creating your database. Organizing data is also one of the most important steps in creating a database because thorough planning helps minimize the amount of retrofitting required after you have started using the database. Modifying the data to be included in a database table after you have already entered data can be time-consuming and can also result in lost data as well as data errors.

In most cases, determining the tables required for a database and identifying the data each table should contain is a relatively simple process. By looking at the information you want to be able to pull from the database, you can quickly identify what data you need to add to the database. From there, logical groupings of data often become evident.

For example, if you were to think about all the pieces of information contained in a hospital bill, you can easily identify some of the data to include in a database.

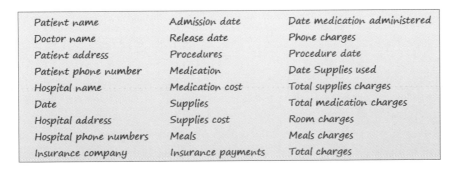

Patient name	Admission date	Date medication administered
Doctor name	Release date	Phone charges
Patient address	Procedures	Procedure date
Patient phone number	Medication	Date Supplies used
Hospital name	Medication cost	Total supplies charges
Date	Supplies	Total medication charges
Hospital address	Supplies cost	Room charges
Hospital phone numbers	Meals	Meals charges
Insurance company	Insurance payments	Total charges

A quick review of these pieces of data shows that it could be organized into the following six tables.

Patients	Hospital	Doctors	Supplies	Medication	Insurance
Patient name	Hospital name	Doctor name	Supply item	Medicine name	Insurance company
Patient address	Hospital address	Doctor address	Supply cost	Medication cost	Insurance address
Patient phone	Hospital phone	Doctor phone	Date supply used	Date medication administered	Insurance payment
Admission date	Room charges	Procedure performed	Total supplies charges	Total medication charges	
Release date	Meals	Procedure date			
	Phone charges				

So careful planning is the first step in creating a database that is both functional and efficient. From this initial planning, you can begin exploring Microsoft Access 2010 and put your planning into action.

Storing Your Exercise Files

Throughout this book, you will be referred to files in your "file storage location." You can store your exercise files on various media, such as on a USB flash drive, in the Documents folder, or to a network drive at a school or company. While some figures may display files on a USB flash drive, it is assumed that you will substitute your own location for that shown in the figures. See Storing Your Exercise Files for additional information on alternative storage media. Storing Your Exercise Files is available on the student web page for this book at labyrinthelab.com/acc10.

 In Windows XP, the folder is called My Documents. In Windows Vista and Windows 7, it is called Documents. Throughout this book we will use the word Documents when referring to this folder.

If you have not yet copied the student exercise files to your local file storage location, follow the instructions in Storing Your Exercise Files, located on the student web page for this book.

1.2 Exploring the Access Environment

Video Lesson labyrinthelab.com/videos

When you launch Access 2010, one of the first things you will notice is that, unlike other Microsoft Office applications, Access displays the Backstage view rather than a new blank file. From the Backstage view, you can create a new database or open an existing one.

Launching Access 2010

The basic procedures for launching Access 2010 are the same as those procedures used to launch other Microsoft Office applications. After you launch Access, you are prompted to take action to create or open a database. These procedures may vary somewhat, depending on the version of Windows installed on your computer as well as whether Access has been used on the computer or not.

DEVELOP YOUR SKILLS 1.2.1
Launch Access 2010

In this exercise, you will launch Access 2010 from the Start menu.

Before You Begin: Navigate to the student web page for this book at labyrinthelab.com/acc10 and see the Downloading the Student Exercise Files section of Storing Your Exercise Files for instructions on how to retrieve the student exercise files for this book and to copy them to your file storage location.

1. Follow these steps to display the All Programs list on the Start menu:

Ⓐ Click the **Start button.**

Calculator

Microsoft FrontPage

▶ All Programs ————— Ⓑ **Choose All Programs.**

Search programs and files 🔍

2. Follow these steps to launch Microsoft Access 2010:

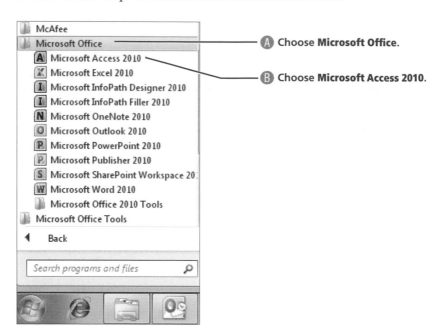

Choose **Microsoft Office**.

Choose **Microsoft Access 2010**.

In future lessons, a Start menu command like this will be written as: Choose All Programs→ Microsoft Office→Microsoft Office Access 2010.

After you launch Access for the first time, the program may appear on the Start menu. You can launch Access directly from the Start menu rather than displaying the menus from the All Programs list.

1.3 Identifying Elements of the Access Window

Video Lesson labyrinthelab.com/videos

Access, unlike other Microsoft Office applications, displays the Backstage view each time you launch it. From this screen, you can choose to create a new database, open an existing database, or open a sample database.

Access commands enable you to create a new database or open an existing one.

The banner provides search tools for locating templates online.

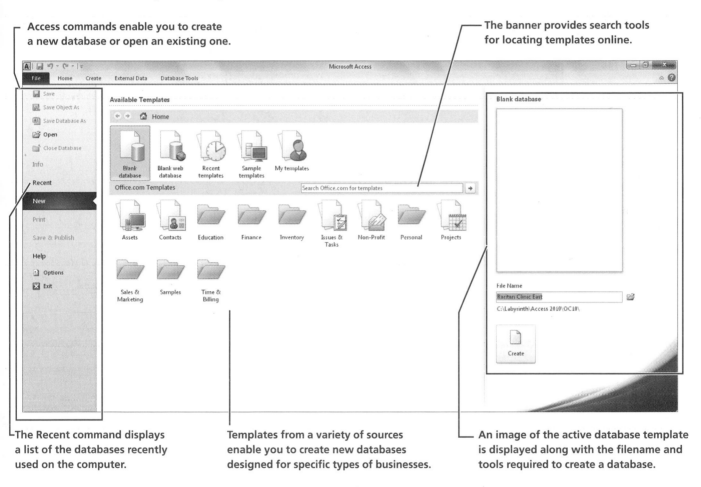

The Recent command displays a list of the databases recently used on the computer.

Templates from a variety of sources enable you to create new databases designed for specific types of businesses.

An image of the active database template is displayed along with the filename and tools required to create a database.

Creating a Blank Database

An electronic database file serves as a shell that holds all the tools, data, and various database objects that help users enter and organize data and obtain meaningful information from that data. As a result, you must save the empty database shell and give it a name as you create it. After you create a new database, Access automatically creates a blank table named Table1.

Create a Blank Database

In this exercise, you will create a new blank database named Raritan Clinic East.

1. Launch **Access 2010** and follow these steps to create and name the new database:

Ⓐ Click the **Blank Database** icon in the Available Templates section of the Access window. ⎯

Ⓑ Click the **File Name** text box and type **Raritan Clinic East**.

Ⓒ Click the **folder** button to open the File New Database dialog box.

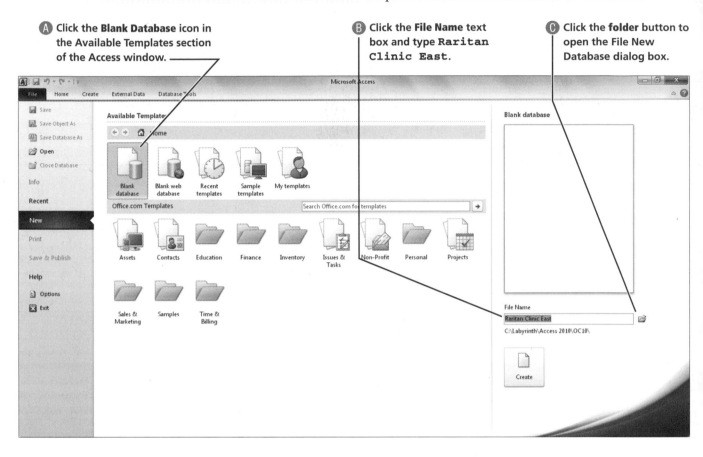

2. Follow these steps to store the database in the appropriate location:

Ⓐ **Navigate to the Lesson 01 folder in which to store your files.**

Ⓑ Click OK.

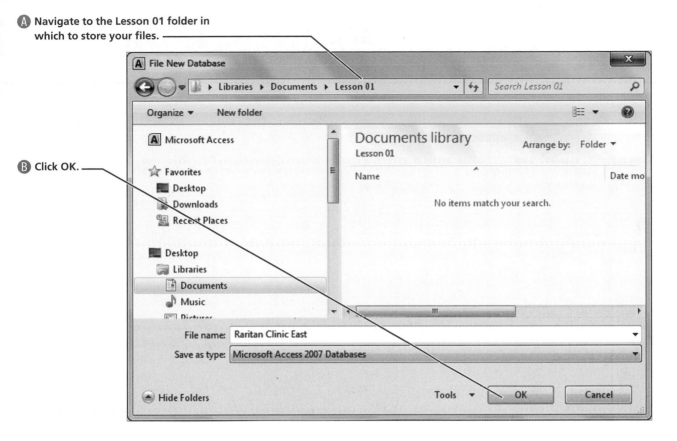

3. Click the **Create** button.

Access creates the new database, shows the database name in the application title bar, and displays a blank table named Table1 in the Access window.

1.4 Identifying Features of the Database Window

Video Lesson labyrinthelab.com/videos

Now that you have created the database file, take a moment to study the layout of the window and compare the visual elements of the window with the features you have seen in other Microsoft Office applications.

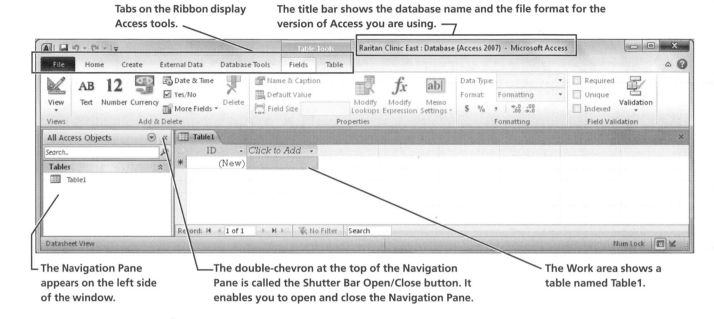

Tabs on the Ribbon display Access tools.

The title bar shows the database name and the file format for the version of Access you are using.

The Navigation Pane appears on the left side of the window.

The double-chevron at the top of the Navigation Pane is called the Shutter Bar Open/Close button. It enables you to open and close the Navigation Pane.

The Work area shows a table named Table1.

Using the Navigation Pane

If you have used Microsoft Office Excel, you know that navigating within a worksheet or workbook is different from navigating within paragraphs of a document. Navigating within an Access database is also different from navigating in a document. As you begin working with the database, some basic procedures for using the Navigation Pane will enable you to navigate the file more efficiently.

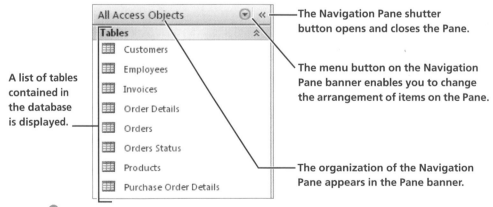

A list of tables contained in the database is displayed.

The Navigation Pane shutter button opens and closes the Pane.

The menu button on the Navigation Pane banner enables you to change the arrangement of items on the Pane.

The organization of the Navigation Pane appears in the Pane banner.

For new databases, a Search bar also appears on the Navigation Pane, just below the Pane banner.

Identifying Object Types

The current database holds only one table. As a result, the Navigation Pane displays only that table. When you have a fully developed database, the Navigation Pane will display all database contents grouped by type of *object*. In Access, an object is an item contained in a database that is designed to serve a specific purpose in the database. The most common object types and their functions in the database are identified in the following table.

ACCESS DATABASE OBJECT TYPES	
Object	**Description**
Tables	The basic objects in a database that contain the data used in all other database objects. Tables hold the data and are also used as input objects because you can use the tables to add data to a database.
Forms	Objects used to display and input data in a layout that is more aesthetically pleasing than table layout while safeguarding other records and improving data integrity.
Reports	Objects in Access databases that process table data and present the data as meaningful information. Reports are output objects.
Queries	Objects used to retrieve data contained in tables on the basis of specific criteria and conditions.

Objects on the Navigation Pane are grouped according to object type. You can expand and collapse each object list to view each object type. You can also select an object from the Navigation Pane banner to display only one object type.

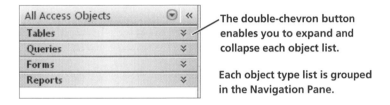

The double-chevron button enables you to expand and collapse each object list.

Each object type list is grouped in the Navigation Pane.

A down-pointing double-chevron indicates that the object list is collapsed and can be expanded; an up-pointing double-chevron indicates that the object list is expanded and can be collapsed.

Customizing the Navigation Pane Menu

The arrangement of items on the Navigation Pane menu is set when the database is created. Because those who use databases work differently, Access provides a variety of arrangements for displaying database items. These arrangements can vary from database to database to contain arrangements unique to the database; however, options to display database objects by type, date created,

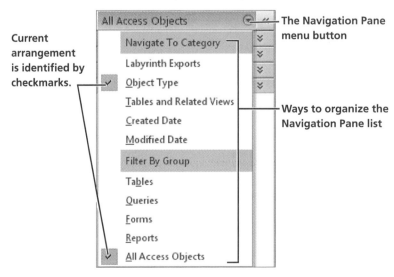

Current arrangement is identified by checkmarks.

The Navigation Pane menu button

Ways to organize the Navigation Pane list

and date modified are standard. In addition to selecting the arrangement of objects, the menu contains tools that enable you to display one list of objects at a time.

Use the Navigation Pane

In this exercise, you will hide and display the Navigation Pane, expand and collapse object lists, and display the Navigation Pane menu.

1. Click the **Collapse** ⊼ button for the Tables group.
The expand button will appear for all object types as you build your database.

2. Follow these steps to change the display of objects in the Raritan Clinic East database Navigation Pane:

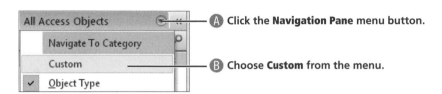

Ⓐ Click the **Navigation Pane** menu button.

Ⓑ Choose **Custom** from the menu.

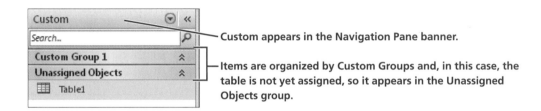

Custom appears in the Navigation Pane banner.

Items are organized by Custom Groups and, in this case, the table is not yet assigned, so it appears in the Unassigned Objects group.

3. Click the **Navigation Pane menu** ⊙ button, and then choose **Object Type** to return the Navigation Pane display to its original format.
The Navigation Pane returns to its All Access Objects display.

1.5 Creating Tables in Datasheet View

Video Lesson   labyrinthelab.com/videos

As you have already learned, all data stored in a database is stored in tables. As a result, Access creates a table for each new database you create, identifies the object using a generic table number (Table1), and creates one field named ID. Access also displays the Table Tools Fields and Table Ribbons so that the tools you need as you build the first table are available. When a database object is active, Access automatically places new Ribbon tabs at the right end of the Tab bar to make accessing appropriate tools more efficient.

Table Tools are distributed on two tabs.

Before you begin building your first table, there are some terms and rules you need to know about tables.

Working with Tables

A database table is the basic object of any database because tables store all of the raw data placed into the database. All other objects in a database are based on data stored in tables. In most databases, you will find a number of tables, each of which holds data related in some way to data in other tables in the database.

Three key terms are used in relation to the data stored in Access databases:

- **Field**—The basic unit of database tables that holds one piece of data, such as first name, last name, street address, ZIP code, date of birth, and so forth. Each field is displayed by a table column.

- **Record**—A collection of all fields related to one item, such as all fields of data for each person or company, all items placed on an order, and personnel information for each employee. Each record appears on a table row.

- **File**—A collection of all related records stored together, such as all employee records found in a table, all customers, all suppliers, and so forth. Each field and record contained in a database table along with forms, reports, and queries used to input data and retrieve meaningful information make up a database file.

Tables are most commonly displayed in the Datasheet View that presents data from multiple records in the column/row layout shown in Table1. As you review the following sample table and work with tables, you will see how these elements fit together.

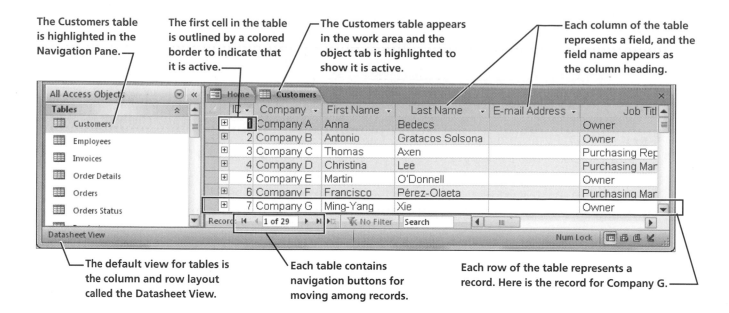

The Customers table is highlighted in the Navigation Pane.

The first cell in the table is outlined by a colored border to indicate that it is active.

The Customers table appears in the work area and the object tab is highlighted to show it is active.

Each column of the table represents a field, and the field name appears as the column heading.

The default view for tables is the column and row layout called the Datasheet View.

Each table contains navigation buttons for moving among records.

Each row of the table represents a record. Here is the record for Company G.

Identifying Table Guidelines

If you are acquainted with the Microsoft Word table feature or Microsoft Excel worksheets, you will find using the Access datasheet familiar. Because tables hold the field names and data used in other database objects, tables must be created first in Access databases.

Each table in the Raritan Clinic East database will contain fields that focus on specific data—patients, supplies, employees, etc. As you build the tables for the database, consider these guidelines:

- Each table should have a *primary key* field that contains unique data—data that will not be the same for any two database records. Social Security Numbers make a good example of unique data because no two people have the same number; however, most organizations have avoided using Social Security Numbers for security reasons. As a result, most organizations use some type of coded ID such as employee number, patient number, or item number as primary keys.

- As you have discovered in the database you just created, Access creates the first field (ID) for you when you create a new database. It uses this field as a primary key field designed to hold unique data. To ensure that the data is unique, Access will assign sequential numeric values to each record you enter. You can leave the field as Access presents it or change the ID field to a different field name, depending on how your table is set up.

- The field identified as the primary key field must contain data—it cannot be empty. When Access creates the primary key field, it automatically sets the key field to automatically number the records. This ensures that each record has a unique number.

- Planning database tables to share data before you add them to the database reduces the amount of time spent editing and restructuring the tables.

- Tables have at least one field in common with another database table so that you can tie together information between any two tables to create reports and other database objects. These common fields are sometimes referred to as *foreign keys*. In an Employees table, the EmployeeNumber might tie it to the Customers table and serve as a foreign key.

Identifying Reserved Words

Access contains a list of specific words that it considers *reserved* words. Reserved words have special meaning for Access or for the Microsoft database engine. If you use these words as field names or objects names, you may receive an error message advising you that the word is a reserved word. Reserved words may be used in conjunction with other words as field names as long as the reserved word is connected without spaces to another word in the field name.

One example of a reserved word is the word *name*. When used alone as a field name, Access displays an error message telling you that it cannot be used because it is reserved. When used as part of another word, such as *FirstName*, however, Access accepts the field name.

For a complete list of reserved words, search the internet for reserved words and review the list.

Requiring Data in Key Fields

The field identified as the primary key field must contain data—it cannot be empty. When Access creates the primary key field, it automatically sets the key field to automatically number the records. This ensures that each record has a unique number. Businesses create a coding system for customers, accounts, and other types of data and rely on this data to be the key field.

The Primary Key button on the Table Tools→Design→Tools Ribbon enables you to assign a primary key to any field containing unique data.

Identifying Field Data Types

As you access each column in a new table datasheet, Access displays a drop-down list that enables you to identify the type of data you plan to place in the field. When you think about the data you plan to enter for a field, it's easy to see the different types of data—text, currency, dates, and so forth. By defining the type of data each field will contain, Access formats the data to some degree, and reduces the amount of formatting you must apply as you enter the data. A description of data types available for data in Access 2010 databases appears in the following table:

QUICK REFERENCE	IDENTIFYING ACCESS DATA TYPES
Data Type	**Description**
Text	The default data type that contains up to 255 characters consisting of any combination of alphabetic and numeric characters—such as names, addresses, and phone numbers—that will not be used to perform calculations.
Memo	Text entries that contain between 1 and 63,999 characters.
Number	Numeric data to be used in mathematical calculations.
Date & Time	Fields that hold date and time values.
Currency	Numeric values representing dollars and cents or fields in which you want to prevent rounding off during calculations.
AutoNumber	A field for which Access assigns a unique, sequential, or random number as records are added to a table. AutoNumber data cannot be modified or deleted.

Data Type	Description
Yes/No	Single-character entries in a Yes/No format that are used to enter data that can be only one of two possible values, such as true/false, yes/no, or on/off.
Hyperlink	Links to web pages or other documents that you access by clicking the link.
Attachment	A data type that identifies any type of file—such as a document, an image, and so forth—that will be included in the database as an attachment.
Lookup & Relationship	A field that displays values from another table or from a list of values on the basis of *criteria*—conditions you set so that you can select the value you want to enter.
Calculated Field	A field created by combining values in other fields within the table.

Saving Tables

Each object you create in a database must be saved. As you save the database objects, you assign an appropriate name to the object. An appropriate name for each table, then, should help identify the data it holds. After you save the table, Access displays the name you give the table in the Navigation Pane.

DEVELOP YOUR SKILLS 1.5.1

Create and Save a Table Using a Datasheet

In this exercise, you will create a table to hold Raritan Clinic East employee data.

1. Choose **Create→Tables→Table**.

2. **Double-click** the ID field column heading to select the text and type **EmployeeNumber**.

3. **Press** Tab and then follow these steps to add a field name for column 2:

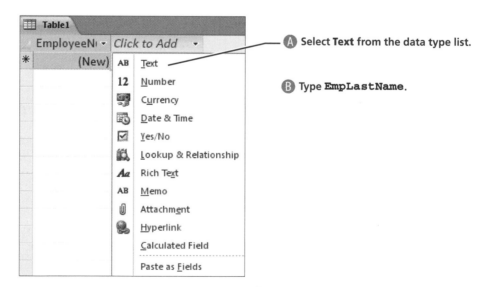

(A) Select **Text** from the data type list.

(B) Type **EmpLastName**.

Notice the underlined mnemonic character identified for each data type. As you enter access each column heading and prepare to set the data type, you can use the mnemonic character (such as T for Text) to select the data type and then type the field name.

Field names/column headings truncate because the columns are narrow.

4. **Press** Tab and repeat the procedures outlined in **step 2** to enter the following text fields in the order indicated by the letters:

    a. EmpFirstName   b. EmpStreet

    c. EmpCity   d. EmpState

    e. EmpZIP   f. EmpTelephone

5. Repeat the procedures outlined in **step 2** to add the following three date fields to the datasheet, ensuring that Date & Time is the data type.

    a. EmpDateHired   b. EmpTermDate

    c. EmpDOB

6. Follow these steps to save the table using a new table name:

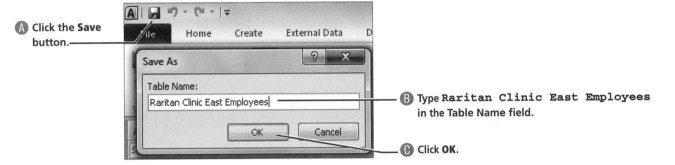

Ⓐ Click the **Save** button.

Ⓑ Type `Raritan Clinic East Employees` in the Table Name field.

Ⓒ Click **OK**.

Navigating Tables and Entering Data

Video Lesson   labyrinthelab.com/videos

Now that the table is complete and saved as the first object in the database, you are ready to enter data into the table fields. Because of the column and row layout of the datasheet, moving from field to field within the datasheet is similar to moving among columns and rows of a Word table or cells in an Excel worksheet:

- Press Tab or Enter to move to the next field.
- Press Shift + Tab to move to the previous field.
- Click a field to make it active.

As you access each field, you simply type the data required for the record. When you complete the data in the last field, pressing Tab or Enter takes you to the first field in the next record. Access saves each record as you complete it, so each new record becomes part of the database table when you move to the next record.

Study the following figure to identify key features of the datasheet as you enter data.

Record/row selector buttons appear on the left side of the datasheet. These buttons enable you to select a record.

As you enter data for a record, a pencil appears in the record/row selector button for the record you are typing.

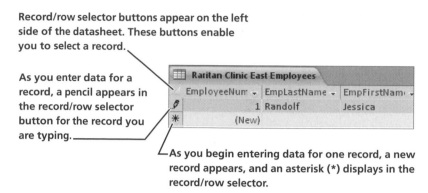

As you begin entering data for one record, a new record appears, and an asterisk (*) displays in the record/row selector.

Using AutoCorrect

As you may already have discovered when using other Microsoft Office 2010 applications, AutoCorrect is a feature that is built into each application. AutoCorrect helps correct common typographical errors as you enter data just as it does when you mistype common words in Word, Excel, Outlook, or PowerPoint. When typing data into database fields, however, detailed data involves acronyms and proper names, so AutoCorrect functions less frequently.

As a shared tool in Microsoft Office applications, any additional settings you add to Auto-Correct are available in Access. As a result, if you have added frequently mistyped words to AutoCorrect while working in Word, they will automatically correct the same mistyped word in Access. You may also find AutoCorrect a useful tool for expanding acronyms so that they type complex phrases or names. For example, you might enter RCE into AutoCorrect so that each time you type RCE and press the spacebar or Enter, Access and other Microsoft Office applications will automatically replace RCE with Raritan Clinic East.

Working with Tabs and Closing Database Objects

As you have already learned, when you create a new database, Access creates a blank table and displays the table in the work area of the database screen. The tab that appears at the top left of the table displays the table name—Table1—until you save the table. Then the name you assign the table appears on the tab.

As you work with Access and build a database, the number of tables and other objects will grow, so you might have numerous objects open at the same time. When multiple objects are open, Access displays as much of each object as will fit within the work area, and all objects are layered, one on top of the other. The tabs make moving from one object to another more efficient.

At the far right side of the table datasheet window, you will notice the table Close button.

Each open object in this database is identified by a tab.

The Close button at the far right of each tabbed object is the object Close button.

DoctorID	DrFirstName	DrLasstName	DrStreet	DrCity	DrState	DrZIP	DrTelephone	DrDateHired	DrDOB	Clic
1	Kayla	Walker	234 Hanson Dr.	San Diego	CA	92126	(714) 555-8934	4/14/2006	3/22/1974	
10	Zachary	Scott	49 Racine	San Diego	CA	92118	(612) 555-7575	8/30/2006	8/2/1945	
11	Jose	Green	55 Raine Rd	San Diego	CA	92126	(609) 555-9000	9/1/2006	3/26/1980	

Enter Data into a Table Datasheet

In this exercise, you will enter data for two records into the Raritan Clinic East table of the Raritan Clinic East database.

1. Follow these steps to enter data into the first two fields of the first record in the table:

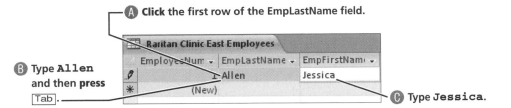

A **Click** the first row of the EmpLastName field.

B Type **Allen** and then **press** **Tab**.

C Type **Jessica**.

2. Continue **pressing** **Tab** to work through the record fields and enter the following values for the first record in the table:

EmpStreet	EmpCity	EmpState	EmpZIP	EmpTelephone	EmpDateHired	EmpDateTerm	EmpDOB
986 Kilsdonk Ct.	San Diego	CA	98109	6195553902	6/12/2006		11/09/1980

3. **Press** **Tab** to create a new record, add your name in the **EmpLastName** and **EmpFirst-Name** fields, and then complete the second record by entering the following data to complete the record:

EmpStreet	EmpCity	EmpState	EmpZIP	EmpTelephone	EmpDateHired	EmpDateTerm	EmpDOB
23 Ida Way	San Diego	CA	92126	6195551470	8/14/2001		11/15/1947

4. **Press** **Tab** or **Enter** after entering data into the last field to ensure that the record is complete.

Video Lesson   labyrinthelab.com/videos

After entering data into a table datasheet, there may be times when you want to print raw data contained in a table datasheet. Access provides tools for printing all of these objects.

Setting Up Data to Print

When you print from a table datasheet, Access prints the data that actually appears in the datasheet when you issue the print command. You can hide columns to prevent them from printing, change the page layout settings to print the datasheet in landscape layout, and change the margins to fit a datasheet on a single sheet of paper as you can when you print documents or spreadsheets.

Examining the Preview Window

Previewing data before you print helps determine adjustments that need to be made to ensure that the datasheet prints on the page as you want it to. You can view multiple pages in print preview to see how columns line up, what columns appear on separate pages, and so forth, so that you can make the necessary adjustments to the datasheet.

Because the layout of database objects differs, options available in the Print dialog box vary depending on what you are printing. However, the basic procedures used to preview and print database objects are the same and are similar to the procedures used to print files in other applications. When you preview an object, the Print Preview tools appear on the Ribbon. These tools are used to change the layout of the page on which you print.

The Print Preview Ribbon contains tools for changing the layout of the printed document.

Preview settings enable you to change the number of pages displayed onscreen at one time.

Close Print Preview restores the access object window.

Navigation buttons enable you to review all pages as they will print.

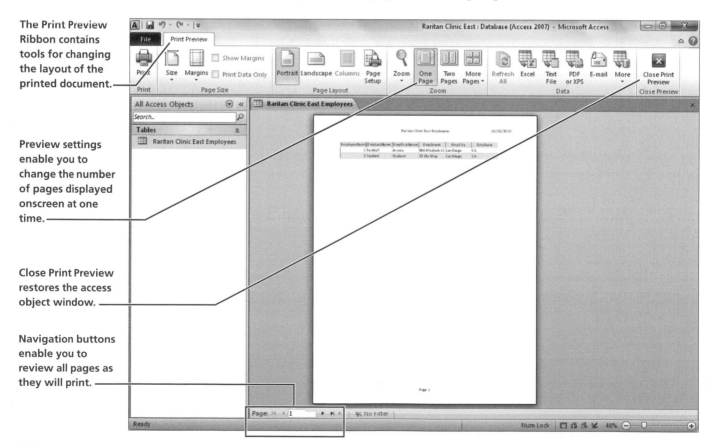

Preview and Print Data

In this exercise, you will preview and print a database table. The Raritan Clinic East table should be open in Access.

1. Follow these steps to preview the datasheet:

A Click the **File** tab.

B Choose **Print** to display the Print menu.

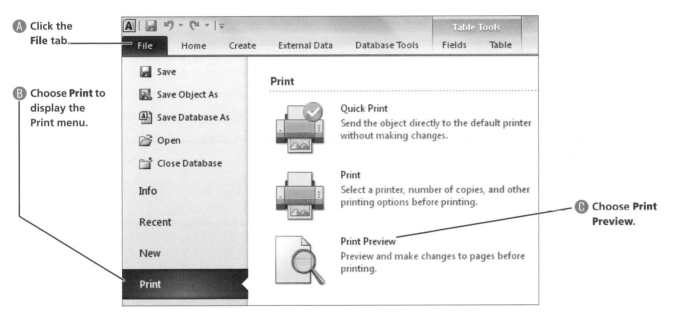

C Choose **Print Preview.**

2. Follow these steps to view pages that will print:

A Click the **Next Page** navigation button and review all pages of the document. As long as the Next Page button is active, another page is required to print the datasheet.

B **Click** the middle of the document text to zoom in on the page.

C Notice that some columns of the datasheet do not display.

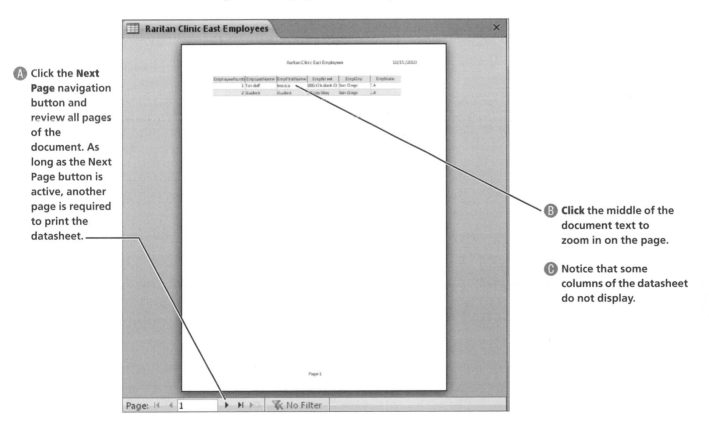

3. Follow these steps to display multiple pages in the preview window:

 A Click the **Two Pages** button to display two pages of the printout together onscreen.

B Click the text on page 2 of the document to zoom in on it.

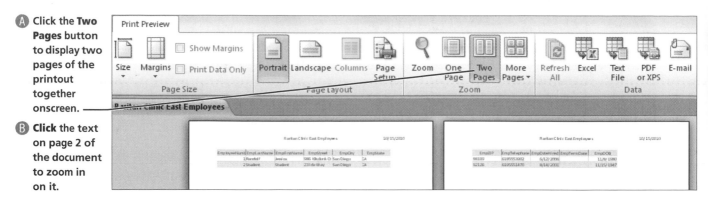

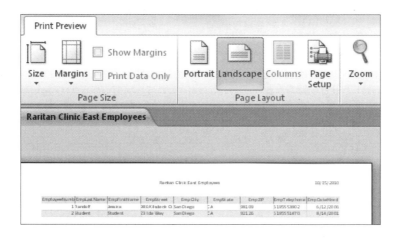

NOTE The appearance of buttons and features on the Ribbon varies depending on screen resolution and size as well as the size of the application window.

4. Choose **Print Preview→Page Layout→Landscape** A⃞ on the Ribbon to display more of the datasheet on one page.

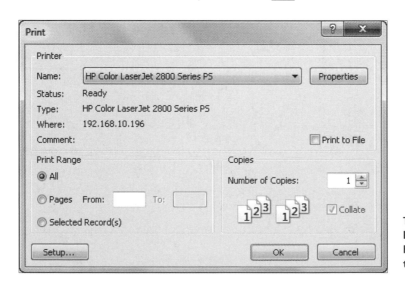

Landscape layout displays more columns together on a sheet.

5. Choose **Print Preview→Print→Print** 🖨 on the Ribbon to open the Print dialog box.

The Print dialog box you see may be different from the one shown here because of the difference in the printer that is active.

6. **Select** options in the Print dialog box to print one copy of all pages; then, either **print** or click **Cancel**.

7. **Close** ☒ the table. Choose **No** when prompted to save changes.

8. **Close** the Navigation Pane.

1.7 Using Help

Video Lesson labyrinthelab.com/videos

Help is a common feature among most Windows-based programs. For Access 2010, much of the Help available is Web-based—that is, when you connect to Help, you are accessing the up-to-date Help system online. By placing its Help system online, Microsoft is able to update the Help files and make these updated files available to users universally. To access Help in Access 2010, use one of the following procedures:

■ Press F1 on the keyboard.
■ Click the Help button ⊚ on the tab bar.

Depending on the program you are using when you access Help, the help files displayed automatically pertain to the active application. As a result, when you access Help from Access 2010, help on Access 2010 topics display.

Access Help and Databases

As you begin using Help in Access 2010, you will soon realize that the Help system is a massive database file composed of numerous records, each of which is related to an Access feature. Using search tools available on most Web sites, you can quickly and efficiently locate help on any Access feature required.

FROM THE KEYBOARD
F1 to launch Help

DEVELOP YOUR SKILLS 1.7.1
Use Help in Access 2010

In this exercise, you will use the Help tool to learn more about AutoCorrect and its use in Access.

1. Click the **Help** ⊚ button on the tab bar to open the Access Help dialog box.

2. Follow these steps to search for help on AutoCorrect:

Ⓐ Type **AutoCorrect** in the text box.   Ⓑ Click **Search**.

3. Click the "Automatically correct spelling and insert text and symbols by u…" as shown in the following figure.

4. Review and **close** the article.
Closing the article also closes the Access Help dialog box.

 The topics listed in the Help window are constantly updated. As a result, the topics listed when you search for help on AutoCorrect will differ from those shown in this activity.

1.8 Closing a Database and Exiting Access

Video Lesson labyrinthelab.com/videos

After all objects in a database are closed, you can close the database and exit Access. The procedures used to perform these tasks are the same as those used to close files and exit other Microsoft Office applications. Use these techniques to close a database and exit Access:

- Choose the File tab and select Close Database to close the database.
- Press [Alt]+[F4] from the keyboard to exit Access.
- Click the File tab and select Exit.
- Click the Access 2010 application window Close [X] button.

Because Access databases contain numerous objects, it is always a good idea to close each database properly before exiting Access. This ensures that all objects in the database are put away carefully.

DEVELOP YOUR SKILLS 1.8.1
Close a Database and Exit Access

In this exercise, you will close the Raritan Clinic East database and exit Access.

1. Choose **File→Close** Database.
2. Click the Access 2010 application window **Close** [X] button.

This lesson provided you with an overview of the basic features and elements related to Access 2010 databases and the basic procedures for creating a database. This sets the foundation for your study of Access. As you progress through your study of Access you will learn more about each element and feature.

1.9 Concepts Review

Concepts Review labyrinthelab.com/acc10

To check your knowledge of the key concepts introduced in this lesson, complete the Concepts Review quiz by going to the URL listed above. If your classroom is using Labyrinth eLab, you may complete the Concepts Review quiz from within your eLab course.

Reinforce Your Skills

Create a New Database with a Table

First Perk is a coffee shop that is getting ready to open in your town. Before opening, they would like to have a database in place that will enable them to track sales, supplies, menu items, etc. In this exercise, you will create the First Perk database and the first table.

1. Launch **Access** and click the **Blank Database** icon.

2. Type **rs-First Perk** in the File Name text box and click the **Browse** folder to select a folder in which to save the database.

3. Choose **Create** to create the database.

4. Change the ID field name to **ItemNumber**, and then **enter** the following field names into the **Table1** column headings, selecting the data type shown for each field:

Field Name	Data Type
ItemName	Text
Price	Currency

5. **Save** the table using the table name **Menu Items**.

6. Add the following records to the **Menu Items** table:

Item Name	Price
Cappuccino	2
Latte	3

7. **Print** a copy of the datasheet and then **close** the database.

Create a School Report Database

Every university and school has a giant database that stores data for students, faculty, classes, grades, and so forth. In this exercise, you will identify fields needed to store student data for such a database and group these fields into appropriate objects.

1. Using a sheet of paper, a document in Word, or an Excel worksheet, list reports that are commonly generated by schools for students.

2. List data fields required to generate the reports for students at your school.

3. Create a **new** database named **NSW University**.

4. Add the following fields for storing data related to classes to the table Access automatically creates:

Field	Data Type
Department	Text
Class Number	Text
Section Number	Text
Building	Text
Room Number	Text
Start Time	Date & Time
End Time	Date & Time
Credit Hours	Number

5. **Save** the table using the table name **Classes**.

6. **Close** the database.

Apply Your Skills

Create a Tech Company Database

Databases have proven to be valuable data storage devices for department stores and other retail businesses because they can store data about employees as well as about suppliers, customers, and orders. In this exercise, you will create a database containing one table for the PriceCo company.

1. Create a **new** blank database named **PriceCo** and store the database with your student files.

2. **Add** the following fields to the table datasheet:

Field Name	Data Type
FirstName	Text
LastName	Text
Street	Text
City	Text
State	Text
ZIP	Text
Telephone	Text
District	Text

3. **Save** the table using the table name **Customers**.
   Leave the database open for the next exercise.

Enter Data and Print Datasheet Data

The Customers table is now ready for data. In this exercise, you will enter data into the Customers table and print a copy of the data.

1. **Enter** the following records into the Customers table in the PriceCo database:

FirstName	LastName	Street	City	State	ZIP	Telephone
Ryan	Manford	12 E. MacArthur	Sacramento	CA	97609	916-555-7523
Earl	Kelly	77 Kingfisher	Salinas	CA	98123	831-555-1368
Jacob	Jones	4323 NW 63rd	Rogers	AR	72757	501-555-5050

2. **Preview** the datasheet and then **print** a copy of the data.

3. **Close** the database.

Critical Thinking & Work-Readiness Skills

In the course of working through the following Microsoft Office-based Critical Thinking exercises, you will also be utilizing various work-readiness skills, some of which are listed next to each exercise. Go to labyrinthelab.com/ workreadiness to learn more about the work-readiness skills.

1.1 Create a New Database

Raritan Clinic East is exploring expanding the number of items they currently recycle. To determine if there are additional ways they can recycle, the clinic administrators have asked James Elliott to do some research about recycling in the community. To help James, go online and determine whether your state has information about recycling in the state. Create a new database named **ct-Recycling in [Your State]** that contains one table. The table should include fields for recycling locations throughout the state and a contact name for the person in charge of the recycling facility. Enter data for at least three sites/companies listed online. Finally, add a record containing your school as the site/ company and your name as the contact. Print a copy of your table datasheet.

WORK-READINESS SKILLS APPLIED
- Organizing and maintaining information
- Thinking creatively
- Knowing how to learn

1.2 Outline a Database

Service Guild at Raritan Clinic East is a nonprofit organization created to raise money to help adults with disabilities receive proper medical care. They have successfully raised more than $60,000 annually through sponsoring a home tour in the city. They would like a database that will enable them to track membership, donations from businesses, ticket sales, etc. You can help them plan their database by identifying fields and tables that should be included in the database. On a clean sheet of paper, identify sample tables that need to be included in the database and the fields that you would place in each table.

WORK-READINESS SKILLS APPLIED
- Solving problems
- Organizing and maintaining information
- Improving or designing systems

1.3 Use Online Forums Related to Access

James Elliott has found that he needs more information about Access. He has asked you to review online forums to see what those who use Access regularly are discussing. Locate several online forums that cover issues related to Access 2010 and identify the five most frequently discussed topics on each forum. Use these discussion items to create a new database named **ct-Access 2010 Forum Topics** that contains a table in which you can store the topics you have identified, along with the names of the forums you reviewed and the web address of the forum.

WORK-READINESS SKILLS APPLIED
- Knowing how to learn
- Applying technology to a task
- Acquiring and evaluating information

Building a Database

LESSON OUTLINE

2.1   Designing a Database

2.2   Opening a Database

2.3   Saving a Database as a New File

2.4   Opening Database Objects

2.5   Creating Database Objects

2.6   Creating Tables Using Other Techniques

2.7   Creating a New Database Using a Template

2.8   Managing Databases and Database Objects

2.9   Concepts Review

Reinforce Your Skills

Apply Your Skills

Critical Thinking & Work-Readiness Skills

LEARNING OBJECTIVES

After studying this lesson, you will be able to:

- Identify key database design techniques
- Open an existing database
- Create a database table using Design View
- Create a form
- Create a report
- Create a table from an Excel worksheet
- Create a new database using a template

Whether you are creating a new database or working with an existing database, building the database by creating database objects is often required. Successful projects normally start with a list of tasks to accomplish, an outline of the order in which to complete these tasks, and a projected final product. You can apply these same concepts to building a database. Start with a list of data (fields) to include in the database, and then group the fields into objects—tables, forms, reports—required for the database. After these lists are complete, you can sit down at the computer and begin building the database. In this lesson, you will expand the design of a database for Raritan Clinic East, a pediatric diagnostic and treatment clinic. You will add a new table, a form, and a report to the database. In addition, you will learn alternative ways to create tables in a database and create a new database using a template.

Designing and Building a Database

Dr. Edward Jackson is the chief operating officer of the Raritan Clinic East, a medical practice staffed by clinical diagnosticians in the Pediatric fields of General Medicine, Cardiology, and Orthopedics, Pediatric Emergency Medicine, and Neonatology. The clinic has recently moved to a new location that has state-of-the-art diagnostic equipment and an updated computer system. It is currently in the process of designing and modernizing its database to make it more efficient to use. Dr. Jackson has asked you to work with consultants to design a basic database that can grow with the clinic as the business expands. After reviewing the needs of the clinic and the existing database, you will add a table, a form, and a report to the database. You will then be able to test these objects by adding data to the database table.

Raritan Clinic East

Pediatric Diagnostic Specialists

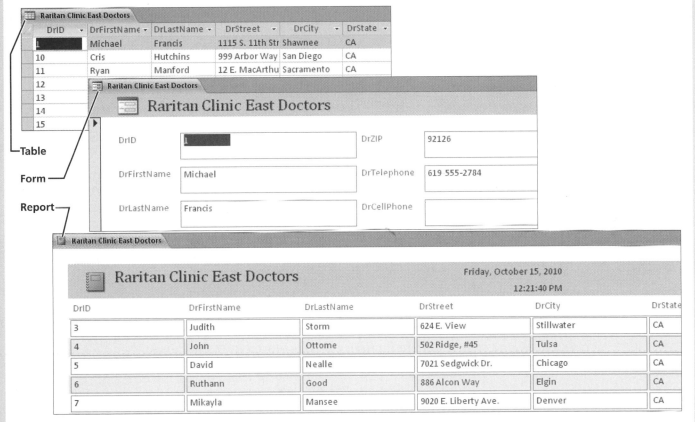

The Raritan Clinic East database will contain a table, a form, and a report. Notice that the icons representing each different object identify the object type.

2.1 Designing a Database

Video Lesson labyrinthelab.com/videos

Creating a database that contains well-organized database objects requires careful planning. Taking the time to sketch out the elements that are required for the database will reduce the amount of time you spend modifying and editing the database design as you start using it.

Planning a Database Design

The mechanics of sitting down at the computer and creating a database are straightforward and reasonably easy—planning the database is often more time consuming. Before sitting down at the computer, answer the following questions about the database you are creating:

- What information do you want to be able to obtain from the database? This information identifies the reports you will add to the database. Reports provide great insight into the fields you need to include in the database tables.

- What data elements (fields) do you need to include in the database to be able to obtain the information?

- What types of data will you enter into each field: dates, numeric values, amounts of money, text, etc.?

- What fields of data relate to the same basic item and could be grouped together? These form the tables.

- How do the groups of data relate to one another? These are the fields that connect the tables to one another.

- What is the most efficient way to get data into the database tables? The answers to this question help you identify the forms required.

- What questions will you need the database to be able to answer? Answers here will identify the queries you need.

Documenting a Database Design

Listing the fields required for a database leads naturally to organizing and grouping the fields into tables that build into forms, queries, and reports. The list you create as you plan the database is often called the *data dictionary* because it identifies and defines each field and the objects in which the field is used within the database. Most databases contain multiple tables. Designing the database to distribute the fields into logical groups helps you define the tables you will need and reduces the redundancy of data stored in the database.

The list on the left shows a brief data dictionary that contains a selected list of fields required for the *Raritan Clinic East* database.

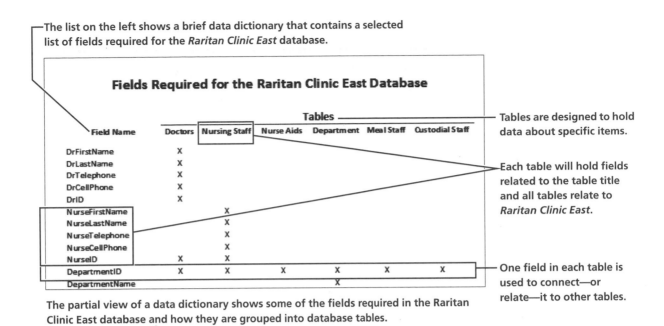

Fields Required for the Raritan Clinic East Database

		Tables				
Field Name	Doctors	Nursing Staff	Nurse Aids	Department	Meal Staff	Custodial Staff
DrFirstName	X					
DrLastName	X					
DrTelephone	X					
DrCellPhone	X					
DrID	X					
NurseFirstName		X				
NurseLastName		X				
NurseTelephone		X				
NurseCellPhone		X				
NurseID	X	X				
DepartmentID	X	X	X	X	X	X
DepartmentName				X		

Tables are designed to hold data about specific items.

Each table will hold fields related to the table title and all tables relate to *Raritan Clinic East.*

One field in each table is used to connect—or relate—it to other tables.

The partial view of a data dictionary shows some of the fields required in the Raritan Clinic East database and how they are grouped into database tables.

2.2 Opening a Database

Video Lesson labyrinthelab.com/videos

The procedures for opening an existing file in Access 2010 are basically the same as those found in other Microsoft Office applications. You can choose one of the following procedures:

■ Choose File→New and select the file from the list of recently used databases on the File menu in Backstage view.

■ Choose File→Open to display the Open dialog box, navigate to the folder containing the file, and open it.

■ Choose File→Recent to display a list of databases in Backstage view.

Enabling Macros Controlling Database Security

Many database files contain *macros*—programming codes that automate common tasks. Because Access 2010 is highly security-conscious, settings that may be active within Access prevent these macros from running without your "permission." The files you use throughout this book have been checked before posting on the website and scanned for viruses, so it's okay to open them and enable database content. If security settings in Access 2010 on your system are set above "low," a message bar appears just below the Ribbon onscreen when you open files. Its presence notifies you of disabled content and provides instructions on how to proceed. When you click the *Enable Content* button, all features of the database operate as intended.

Enable Content button

Setting Trusted Sites

Another way to ensure that the databases you use throughout your study of Access 2010 operate as intended without having to enable the content each time you open the database is to add the folder in which you are storing your files to the Trusted Sites list. Setting the folder as a trusted site instructs Access that the folder and all databases contained in the folder and subfolders are safe, so Access automatically enables content.

DEVELOP YOUR SKILLS 2.2.1

Open a Database, Enable Content, and Set Trusted Site

In this exercise, you will open an existing database, enable the content for the database, and add the folder containing your student data files to the Trusted Sites list.

Open a Database

1. Launch **Access 2010** and choose **File→Open**.

2. Follow these steps to open the Raritan Clinic East database:

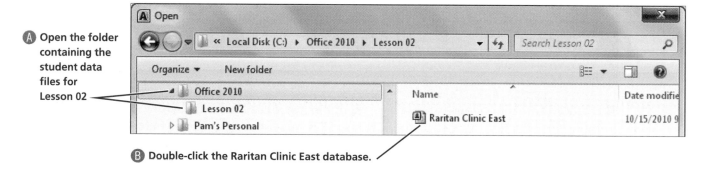

Ⓐ Open the folder containing the student data files for Lesson 02

Ⓑ Double-click the Raritan Clinic East database.

Enable Content

3. Click the **Enable Content** button on the Security Warning bar just below the Ribbon.

Set Trusted Site

4. Choose **File→Options** to open the Access Options dialog box.

5. Follow these steps to open the trust center settings:

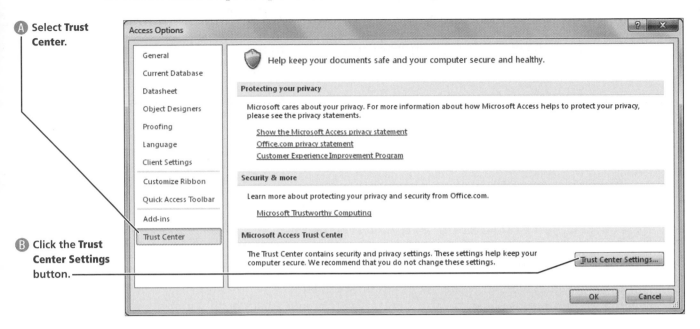

A Select **Trust Center.**

B Click the **Trust Center Settings** button.

6. Follow these steps to add a new folder to the Trust Center:

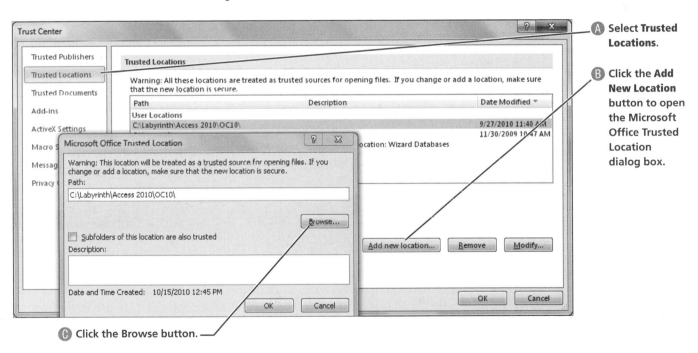

A Select **Trusted Locations.**

B Click the **Add New Location** button to open the Microsoft Office Trusted Location dialog box.

C Click the Browse button.

7. Navigate to the folder containing your student data files, **select** the folder, and click **OK**.

8. Click **OK** to close the Microsoft Office Trusted Location dialog box.

9. Click **OK** to close the Trust Center dialog box.

10. Click **OK** to close the Access Options dialog box.

2.3 Saving a Database as a New File

Video Lesson labyrinthelab.com/videos

As you work with data in database objects, Access saves the data when you move to a new or different record. As a result, you will want to preserve the original student data file as a new database so that the original is available for reuse, if needed. Creating a new database file helps to prevent unwanted loss of data. Access automatically saves each database record as you enter it and also prompts you to save each object as you modify or change it in any way. As a result, the data stored in a database saves regularly as you work. Existing files often make good files on which to create new files.

Using the Save As Command

You can use the File→Save Database As command to save an existing database as a new database using a different filename just as you would with any other Microsoft Office application. Saving a database as a new file is not only a good way to quickly create a new database for a different purpose, but it is also a good way to create a backup of your data to protect it. Because many databases contain numerous objects, the File menu also displays a Save Object As command for saving each of the database objects as new objects within the existing database. Review the Backstage view of the Save As commands to identify how saving a database as a new file is different from saving other types of files as new files.

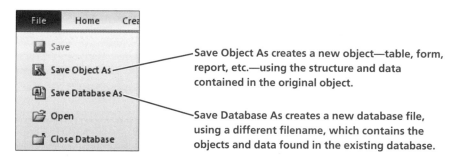

Save Object As creates a new object—table, form, report, etc.—using the structure and data contained in the original object.

Save Database As creates a new database file, using a different filename, which contains the objects and data found in the existing database.

Backstage view of the File menu.

DEVELOP YOUR SKILLS 2.3.1
Save a Database as a New File

In this exercise, you will save the Raritan Clinic East database as a new database file. The Raritan Clinic East database should be open.

1. Choose **File→Save Database As** to open the Save As dialog box.

2. Follow these steps to save the database as a new file:

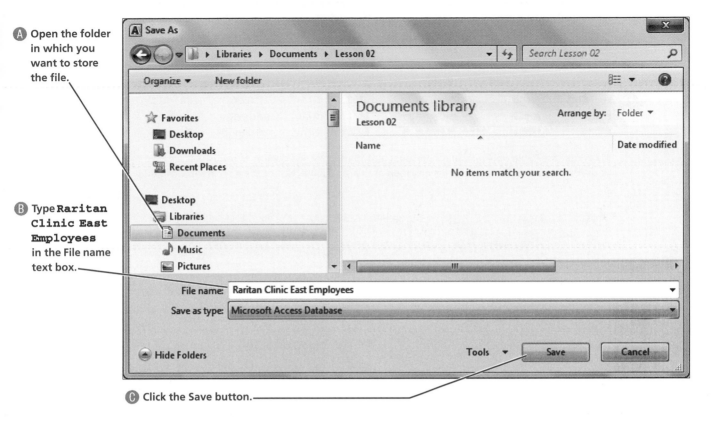

Ⓐ Open the folder in which you want to store the file.

Ⓑ Type **Raritan Clinic East Employees** in the File name text box.

Ⓒ Click the Save button.

2.4 Opening Database Objects

Video Lesson   labyrinthelab.com/videos

As you have most likely already discovered, Access databases contain a variety of different objects to display data and information. Each object in the database is related to other objects in the database. Each type of object in an Access database has a specific purpose. Some objects are used to input data, others are used to store raw data, and still others are used to select and report specific data.

Identifying Database Objects

The four most common objects found in databases include Tables, Forms, Reports, and Queries. Each object type has a different icon to help you identify what type of object it is. The object icon appears in the object tab or title bar, as well as beside each object in the object list. Each object type is identified and described as follows.

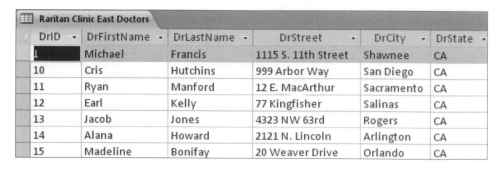

This database Table object displays personal information for the doctors in datasheet view so that data for numerous doctors appears onscreen at the same time. Notice the icon in the table tab.

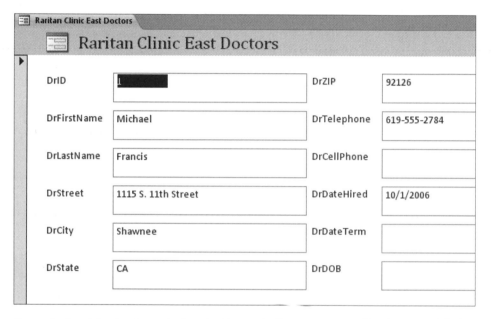

Forms display data about one doctor at a time and offer a more appealing layout and design than the table datasheet view. Notice the form icon in the form tab.

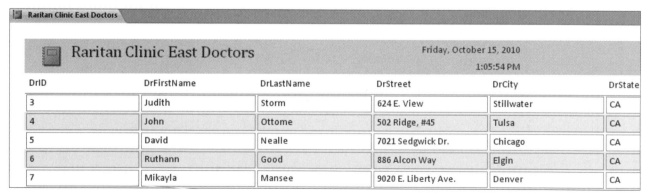

Reports summarize data and display the data as meaningful information.
Notice the report icon in the report tab.

Raritan Clinic East Doctors Query		
DrFirstName ▾	DrLastName ▾	DrTelephone ▾
Michael	Francis	619-555-2784
Cris	Hutchins	619-555-1001
Ryan	Manford	619-555-7523
Earl	Kelly	619-555-1368
Jacob	Jones	619-555-5050
Alana	Howard	619-555-2435

Queries display the columns of data that meet the criteria you set—in a datasheet view. Notice the query icon in the query tab.

QUICK REFERENCE   IDENTIFYING OBJECT TYPES IN ACCESS DATABASES

Object Type	Object Icon	Description
Tables		The basic objects in a database that contain the data used in all other database objects. Tables hold the data and are also used as input objects because you can use the tables to add data to a database.
Forms		Objects used to display and input data in a layout that is more aesthetically pleasing than table layout.
Reports		Objects in Access databases that process table data and present the data as meaningful information. Reports are output objects.
Queries		Objects used to retrieve data contained in tables on the basis of specific criteria and conditions.

Opening Existing Database Objects

Each database object is listed on the Navigation Pane, which groups objects by type. The Raritan Clinic East database contains only one object—a table that lists the doctors who practice at the clinic. Access provides a number of different techniques for opening database objects:

- Double-click the object in the Navigation Pane.
- Right-click the object in the Navigation Pane and choose Open.
- Drag the object name from the Navigation Pane to the Work Area of the Access window.

Opening and reviewing the data contained in a database object is a great way to identify key features of a database.

DEVELOP YOUR SKILLS 2.4.1

Open a Database Table

In this exercise, you will open a table in the Raritan Clinic East Employees database. The Raritan Clinic East Employees database should be open.

1. Click the **Shutter Bar Open/Close Button** ⏩ on the Navigation Pane.
   The Navigation Pane opens with the Tables group collapsed.

2. Click the Tables group **Expand** ⏬ button

3. **Double-click** the Raritan Clinic East Doctors table to open it.

4. Review the data contained in the database table.

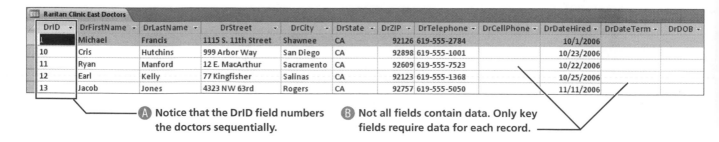

DrID	DrFirstName	DrLastName	DrStreet	DrCity	DrState	DrZIP	DrTelephone	DrCellPhone	DrDateHired	DrDateTerm	DrDOB
	Michael	Francis	1115 S. 11th Street	Shawnee	CA	92126	619-555-2784		10/1/2006		
10	Cris	Hutchins	999 Arbor Way	San Diego	CA	92898	619-555-1001		10/23/2006		
11	Ryan	Manford	12 E. MacArthur	Sacramento	CA	92609	619-555-7523		10/22/2006		
12	Earl	Kelly	77 Kingfisher	Salinas	CA	92123	619-555-1368		10/25/2006		
13	Jacob	Jones	4323 NW 63rd	Rogers	CA	92757	619-555-5050		11/11/2006		

Ⓐ Notice that the DrID field numbers the doctors sequentially.

Ⓑ Not all fields contain data. Only key fields require data for each record.

Navigating Records in a Table Datasheet

Video Lesson   labyrinthelab.com/videos

Tables display many records onscreen at a time. As the number of records in a table grows, however, some records will appear offscreen. Access provides a set of record navigation tools at the bottom of the work area when a table is open. Buttons on the record navigator can be used to move among all records in a table.

DEVELOP YOUR SKILLS 2.4.2
Navigate Records in a Table Datasheet

In this exercise, you will use the record navigator buttons to access various records in the table datasheet. The Raritan Clinic East Doctors should be open in the Raritan Clinic East Employees database.

1. **Press** [Tab] to move to the DrFirstName column.
   You can continue to press [Tab] *to move to the next column (field) until you reach the last column containing data. Pressing* [Tab] *from the last column of the first row (record) moves the cursor to the first column (field) in the second row (record).*

2. Follow these steps to move among table records using table navigation buttons:

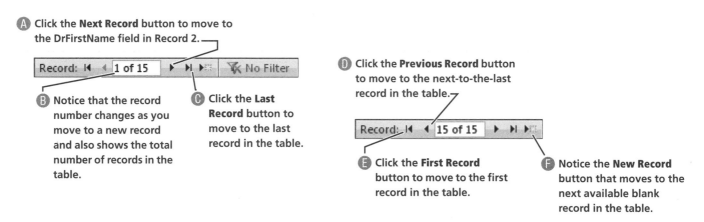

Ⓐ Click the **Next Record** button to move to the DrFirstName field in Record 2.

Ⓑ Notice that the record number changes as you move to a new record and also shows the total number of records in the table.

Ⓒ Click the **Last Record** button to move to the last record in the table.

Ⓓ Click the **Previous Record** button to move to the next-to-the-last record in the table.

Ⓔ Click the **First Record** button to move to the first record in the table.

Ⓕ Notice the **New Record** button that moves to the next available blank record in the table.

3. Click the Raritan Clinic East Doctors table **close** ☒ button to close the table.

2.5 Creating Database Objects

Video Lesson   labyrinthelab.com/videos

As you should already know, all data stored in a database is stored in tables. As a result, Access automatically creates a table when you create a database, identifies the object by type using a generic number (Table1), and creates one field named ID. Access also displays the Table Tools Datasheet tab of the Ribbon so that the tools you need as you enter data into the table are available. Access uses the same object-naming procedure when you create forms, reports, and queries. The name of the object type is sequentially numbered until you save the object using a different object name. Tools for working with each individual object also become available on the Ribbon when you create each object type.

QUICK REFERENCE	CREATING DATABASE OBJECTS
Task	**Procedure**
Create a new database table	■ Display the Create tab on the Ribbon. ■ In the Tables command group on the Ribbon, choose Table.
Create a simple form	■ Choose Create→Forms→Form from the Ribbon.
Create a simple report	■ Choose Create→Reports→Report from the Ribbon.

Creating and Using Forms

Forms are database objects that display table data onscreen one record at a time. Forms serve as input objects for entering data into tables. When you create databases that others will use to enter data, forms are useful data entry objects because they present data fields in a more aesthetically pleasing layout—especially for the novice data entry clerk. Forms gather and display table data. No data is stored in a form.

Identifying Form Tools

Access contains a number of tools that enable you to create forms in different layouts. By applying different form formats, you can make the forms easier to navigate and use to enter data. Tools used to create forms appear on the Create tab of the Ribbon.

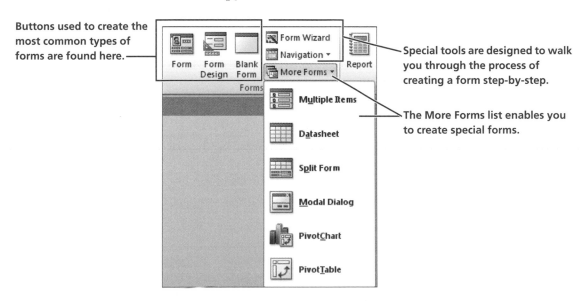

Buttons used to create the most common types of forms are found here.

Special tools are designed to walk you through the process of creating a form step-by-step.

The More Forms list enables you to create special forms.

After you create a form, the Form Layout Tools are available on the Ribbon so that you can modify the form format, if necessary. In this section, you will create a simple form.

Creating Simple Forms

Forms obtain their data and fields from database tables or queries. As a result, it is necessary to select or open the table that contains the fields you want to include on the form. Because queries also use fields stored in database tables, you can also use a query as the object from which to create a form. When you create a form using the Form button on the Create tab of the Ribbon, Access creates a simple form that lists each field contained in the selected or active table. Depending on the number of fields contained in the table, Access displays the fields in a one- or two-column layout starting at the left side of the form. The fields appear in the order in which they appear in the table. Data entry boxes appear in a column on the right parallel to the field names.

Record selection bar used to select a record displayed in a form.

Table field names.

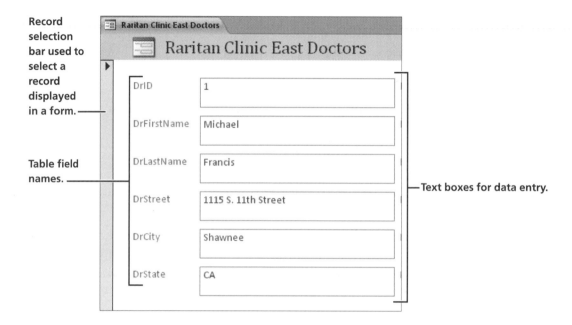

Text boxes for data entry.

DEVELOP YOUR SKILLS 2.5.1

Create a Simple Form

In this exercise, you will create a simple form for entering data for the Raritan Clinic East Doctors table. The Raritan Clinic East Employees database should be open with the Raritan Clinic East Doctors table open as well.

1. Follow these steps to create a form for the Raritan Clinic East Doctors table:

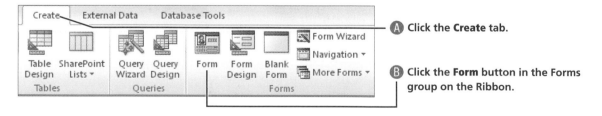

A Click the **Create** tab.

B Click the **Form** button in the Forms group on the Ribbon.

Access creates the new form, names it using the name of the table from which it gets its data, and displays the Form Layout Tools—Design, Arrange, and Format tabs—on the Ribbon.

2. Follow these steps to save the new form:

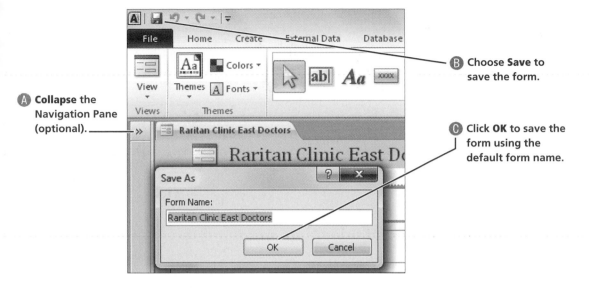

A **Collapse** the Navigation Pane (optional).

B Choose **Save** to save the form.

C Click **OK** to save the form using the default form name.

3. Close ☒ the form. Choose **Yes** to save any changes if prompted.

4. Close ☒ the table.

Entering Data Using Datasheets and Forms

Video Lesson   labyrinthelab.com/videos

Frequently, data entry clerks enter data into only a limited number of table fields. As a result, creating forms that contain only those data entry fields is a valuable tool. The form you created for the Raritan Clinic East Doctors database table contains all the fields included in the Raritan Clinic East Doctors table. You now have two objects in the database to use for entering table data: the table and the form.

After saving and closing forms, Access displays the Home tab of the Ribbon. When a form is open, the View button on the Home tab enables you to switch among the views available for Forms and other objects. Before entering data using the form, you must display the form in Form View. The View button on the Ribbon enables you to change the view of the form you just created so that you can enter data.

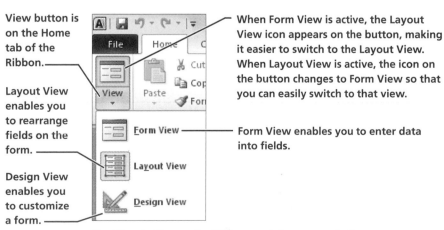

View button is on the Home tab of the Ribbon.

Layout View enables you to rearrange fields on the form.

Design View enables you to customize a form.

When Form View is active, the Layout View icon appears on the button, making it easier to switch to the Layout View. When Layout View is active, the icon on the button changes to Form View so that you can easily switch to that view.

Form View enables you to enter data into fields.

The View button on the Ribbon contains a menu button that displays the views available for the active object.

Using the Record Navigator

Forms display many of the same navigation tools available in tables. The main difference in the display is that records appear onscreen one record at a time. As a result, when you navigate to a specific record, only the data for one item appears. In tables, one record was active as you navigated the table even though multiple records displayed at the same time because of the column and row layout of the tables.

The record navigator appears at the bottom of tables and forms when they are open in the work area. You can use buttons in the record navigator to move to specific records as well as to create a new record.

Record: ◄ ◄ 15 of 15 ► ►► ►⁎ ——New Record button

QUICK REFERENCE	ADDING A NEW RECORD TO A TABLE
Task	**Procedure**
Add a new record to a datasheet	■ Open the table in the database to which you want to add a new record. ■ Click the New Record ►⁎ button to create a new record. ■ Type data into each field in the row, pressing Tab to move to the next field.
Add a new record using a form	■ Open the form associated with the table in the database to which you want to add a new record. ■ Click the New Record ►⁎ button to create a new record. ■ Type data into each field in the form, pressing Tab to move to the next field.

DEVELOP YOUR SKILLS 2.5.2
Add Records to a Table

In this exercise, you will add records to the Raritan Clinic East Doctors table using a form.

1. Open the **Raritan Clinic East Doctors** form.

2. Follow these steps to change the view to ensure that you can enter data:

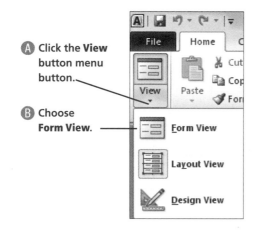

Ⓐ Click the **View** button menu button.

Ⓑ Choose **Form View.**

3. Click the **New Record** button in the Record Navigator area of the status bar.

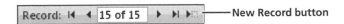
Record: I◄ ◄ 15 of 15 ► ►I ►※ ——New Record button

4. Click the **DrFirstName** field to make it active and follow these steps to enter the values in each form field:

Depending on the settings that are active on your computer, the field arrangement may be different from the one shown here. Be sure to note the field name that is active before typing the data.

Ⓐ Type **Clara** into the DrFirstName text box.

Ⓑ **Press** Enter or Tab **to move to the next field and type the data shown here.**

Ⓒ Continue pressing Enter or Tab to complete the field data in the first column.

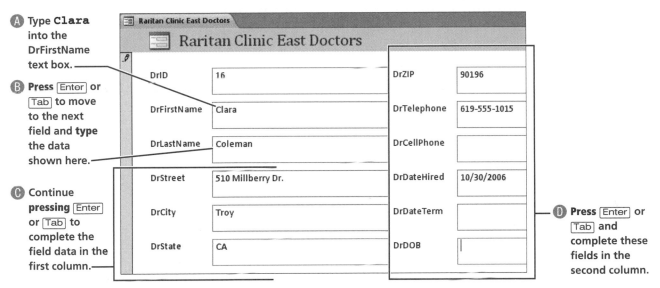

Raritan Clinic East Doctors

DrID	16	DrZIP	90196
DrFirstName	Clara	DrTelephone	619-555-1015
DrLastName	Coleman	DrCellPhone	
DrStreet	510 Millberry Dr.	DrDateHired	10/30/2006
DrCity	Troy	DrDateTerm	
DrState	CA	DrDOB	

Ⓓ **Press** Enter or Tab **and complete these fields in the second column.**

5. **Close** ☒ the table, **saving** changes if prompted.

Creating and Generating Reports

Video Lesson   labyrinthelab.com/videos

While forms are objects used to input data into database tables, reports are database objects used to sort, summarize, and output table data as useful information. Access contains numerous tools designed to help you create new reports. These tools are grouped together on the Create tab in the Report section of the Ribbon, as shown.

Creates a simple report using table fields ——

——Additional tools for creating reports using the Report Wizard, formatted as labels, and starting with a blank report

Creates a report "from scratch" using Access Report Design tools——

As you discovered when you created new forms earlier in this lesson, these tools create reports from the most simple to a more complex report that groups and sorts data. In this lesson, the focus will be on a simple report. After you create a report, the Report Layout Tools—Design, Arrange, Format, and Page Setup—tabs appear on the Ribbon.

Creating a Simple Report

Access contains a Report command that, like the Form tool, helps you create a simple report that lists data from a database table or query. Reports you generate using the Report command contain no data summarization or "frills"—they simply report the data contained in the table, but they report it in a more attractive layout when printed than found by printing the table datasheet.

Identifying Report Views

As you discovered with forms, reports have multiple views that are used to edit the report layout, preview data, or print the report. After you create a report, Access displays the report in Layout View. To view the report as it will print, the report should be displayed in Report view. The Views button appears at the left end of the Ribbon when the Home tab is active to make switching among views more efficient. Report views and their uses are described in the following table.

REPORT VIEWS AND THEIR USES	
Report View	**Description**
Report view	Displays the report onscreen with data displayed.
Print Preview	Displays the report as it will print.
Layout view	Displays a sample of the data in an editable layout that enables you to size and position fields so that all data displays appropriately.
Design view	Displays the report on a palette with field names and placeholders so that you can move and position fields.

DEVELOP YOUR SKILLS 2.5.3
Create a Simple Report

In this exercise, you create a simple report. The Raritan Clinic East Employees database should be open.

1. Follow these steps to create a new report based on data contained in the selected table:

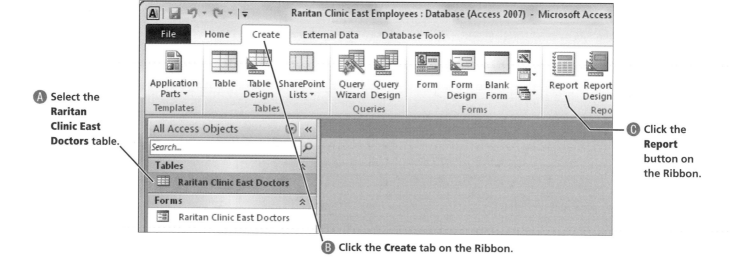

Ⓐ Select the Raritan Clinic East Doctors table.

Ⓑ Click the **Create** tab on the Ribbon.

Ⓒ Click the **Report** button on the Ribbon.

2. Follow these steps to display Report view:

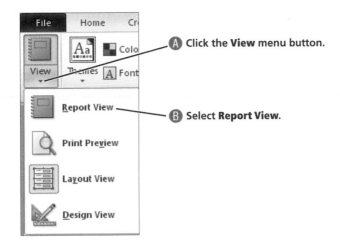

Ⓐ Click the **View** menu button.

Ⓑ Select **Report View**.

3. Review the report and then follow these steps to save the report:

Ⓐ Choose **Save**.

Ⓑ Ensure that Raritan Clinic East Doctors appears in the Report Name text box.

Ⓒ Click **OK**.

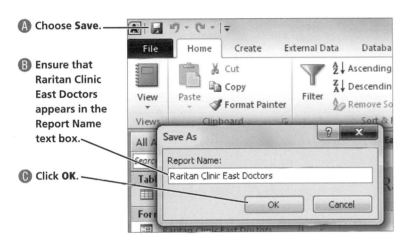

4. **Close** ☒ the report.

Video Lesson labyrinthelab.com/videos

Creating tables using the datasheet to enter field names, set data types, and enter data is a quick and easy way to start building a database. Access makes this even easier by creating a blank table each time you create a new database. You have most likely found with other Microsoft Office applications that there are a number of different ways to create new files. Because Access databases contain a variety of different database objects, Access offers a variety of procedures for creating database objects:

■ Import data from other sources to create a new table

■ Choose Create→Object Type→Object

■ Save an existing object as a new object

■ Import an object from another Access database

Because tables hold the field names and data used in other database objects, tables are normally created first. The database you are building contains only one table—the Raritan Clinic East Doctors table. Now that you have a grasp of the techniques used to create objects, you can begin exploring other techniques for creating tables.

First, you will create a table using Table Design view. You will then create a new table by importing data from Excel and a third table using the Table Wizard.

Displaying and Using Table Design View

When you create a new table in any Access database, Access automatically displays the new table in Datasheet View and assigns a sequentially-numbered generic name to the table. In addition, Access displays the Table Datasheet tools on the Ribbon. When the Design View is active, Access displays the Design tools on the Ribbon. When you switch views during table creation, Access prompts you to save the table if you have not yet done so.

Design graphics appear on the View button to make it easy to switch to Design view.

Data types can be applied to fields added to the datasheet using the Data Type drop-down list.

Tools available on the Ribbon when the Datasheet view is active

When the Design View is active, a datasheet graphic appears on the View button to switch back to Datasheet view.

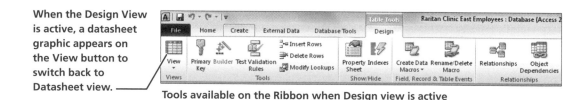

Tools available on the Ribbon when Design view is active

Entering Field Names in Design View

In old-school databases, field names could contain only alphabetic and numeric characters with no spaces, punctuation, or extraneous symbols, and could only be up to eight characters in length. As a result, field names were abbreviated so dramatically that it was often a challenge to determine exactly what data the field would contain. In modern databases, field names can contain all spaces and symbols, except slashes (\ /), wildcard characters (* and ?), and periods. It is also important to remember reserved words. If you have not yet taken the time to review the list of reserved words, this might be a good time to do so.

Because some mainframe systems require the old-school format for naming fields, many database designers still use abbreviated field names with no spaces, punctuation, or symbols. The tables and other objects you create in the Raritan Clinic East Employees database are new-world format to make them easier for you to identify.

Identifying Field Data Types

You may already be familiar with the different types of data entered into database tables and be aware of how to set the data type for each field you add to a table. If not, reviewing the data that you plan to enter into each field will help you determine what type of data the field will contain—text, currency, dates, and so forth. By defining the type of data each field will contain, Access formats the data to some degree, and reduces the amount of formatting you must apply as you enter the data. A description of data types available in Design view for data in Access 2010 databases appears in the following table.

QUICK REFERENCE	IDENTIFYING ACCESS DATA TYPES
Data Type	**Description**
Text	The default data type that contains up to 255 characters consisting of any combination of alphabetic and numeric characters—such as names, addresses, and phone numbers—that will not be used to perform calculations.
Memo	Text entries that contain between 1 and 63,999 characters.
Number	Numeric data to be used in mathematical calculations.
Date/Time	Fields that hold date and time values.
Currency	Numeric values representing dollars and cents or fields in which you want to prevent rounding off during calculations.
AutoNumber	A field for which Access assigns a unique, sequential, or random number as records are added to a table. AutoNumber data cannot be modified or deleted.
Yes/No	Single-character entries in a Yes/No format that are used to enter data that can be only one of two possible values, such as true/false, yes/no, or on/off.
OLE Object	Embedded or linked objects—such as Microsoft Excel spreadsheets, Microsoft Word documents, pictures, sounds, and so forth—that have a storage limit of one gigabyte.
Hyperlink	Links to web pages or other documents that you access by clicking the link.
Attachment	A data type that identifies any type of file—such as a document, an image, and so forth—that will be included in the database as an attachment.
Calculated Field	A field created by combining values in other fields within the table.
Lookup Wizard	A field that displays values from another table or from a list of values on the basis of *criteria*—conditions you set so that you can select the value you want to enter.

Notice that the most commonly used data types all begin with a different first letter. To set a data type other than text, typing the first character of the data type is usually all that is required. For example, to set a Date/Time data type for a field, type D and Date/Time automatically appears.

Entering Descriptions

Descriptions added to each field in a table help those who must use or maintain the database to identify special information about a field. For example, suppose you set up a special coding procedure for the Patient ID field. Entering the plan and coding process for the field can be helpful to those who enter data as well as to those who might eventually have to modify the table design.

Setting Field Properties

As you define each field in a database table, Access sets properties for the field that control the number of characters the field can contain as well as the format of the data and the type characters that are valid for the field data. You can accept the default properties Access sets or modify the properties. Properties available depend on the data type selected for the field.

Identifying a Primary Key

Each table in a database should have a *primary key* field that contains unique data—data that will not be the same for any two database records. Most organizations use some type of coded ID, such as customer ID or serial number, as primary keys. Each time you create a new table Access creates an ID field and marks the field as the primary key field. You can rename the field, remove the primary key designation from the field and assign it to another field, or leave the field as Access created it. To ensure that the data contained in the field is unique, Access will assign sequential numeric data to each record you enter.

Requiring Data in Key Fields

The field identified as the primary key field must contain data—it cannot be empty. When Access creates the primary key field, it sets the key field to automatically number the records. This ensures that each record has a unique number. Businesses create a coding system for customers, accounts, and other types of data and rely on this data to be the key field.

The Primary Key button on the Design→Tools tab of the Ribbon enables you to assign a primary key to any field containing unique data.

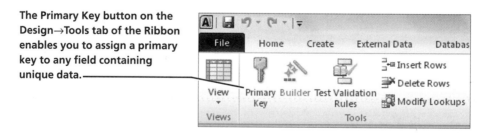

Create a Database Table Using Design View

In this exercise, you will create a new table in the Raritan Clinic East Employees database using Table Design View. The Raritan Clinic East Employees database should be open.

1. Choose **Create→Tables→Table** on the Ribbon to create the new table and then follow these steps to save the table and switch to Design View:

A Choose **Fields→ Views→View→ Design View** to display the Save As dialog box.

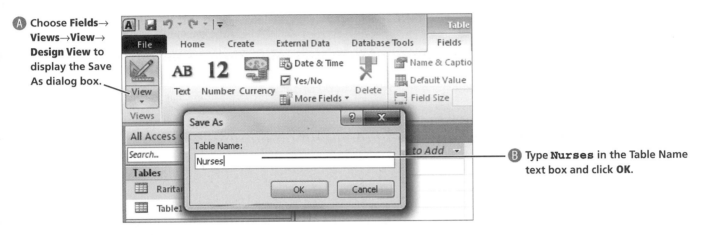

B Type **Nurses** in the Table Name text box and click **OK**.

Access displays the Nurses table in Table Design View. Notice that the ID field is identified as the Primary Key field because the Primary Key button is highlighted to show that it is active. A key icon appears beside the field name in the Field Name list.

2. Follow these steps to create the first table field:

A Click the **ID Field Name**, type **NurseID** in the first row of the Field Name column, and **press** Tab.

B Click the **Data Type** list button and select Text.

C Press Tab and type **Month and year of hire date and last four digits of SS#--8 digits.**

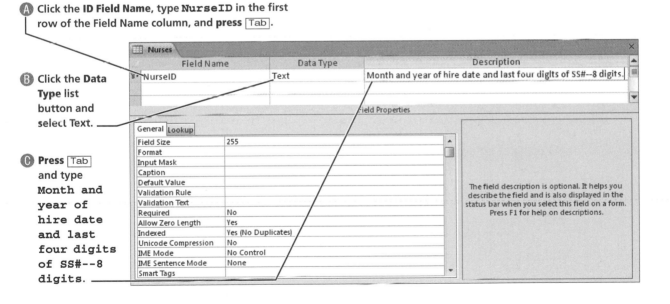

3. **Press** [Tab] and repeat the procedures outlined in **step 2** to enter the following additional fields and field information:

Field Name	Data Type	Description
NrFirstName	Text	
NrLastName	Text	
NrStreet	Text	
NrCity	Text	
NrState	Text	
NrZIP	Text	
NrTelephone	Text	
NrHireDate	Date/Time	Date of first working day
NrTermDate	Date/Time	Date of last working day
NrDOB	Date/Time	

4. **Save** 🖫 the table and **close** ✕ it.

Creating a Table from an Excel Worksheet

Video Lesson   labyrinthelab.com/videos

Sometimes the data you want to use in a database exists in an electronic file created in another application such as Excel. Rather than retype the data, you can retrieve the data from its original file to create a new Access table. This process of retrieving data from other files is called *importing* data. When you import data from other programs, Access examines the file and prompts you for information about the file so that data imports accurately. In the case of an Excel worksheet, Access uses the Import Spreadsheet Wizard to guide the process. After you import the data, it becomes part of the database file. Changes you make to the Excel file have no impact on the table data in Access and vice versa.

The External Data tools on the Ribbon are used to import and export data as well as to collect data and connect to SharePoint lists. Import buttons are grouped on the Ribbon with Linking tools.

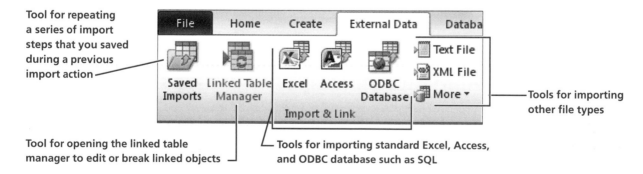

Tool for repeating a series of import steps that you saved during a previous import action

Tool for opening the linked table manager to edit or break linked objects

Tools for importing standard Excel, Access, and ODBC database such as SQL

Tools for importing other file types

DEVELOP YOUR SKILLS 2.6.2

Import Excel Data

In this exercise, you will create the Nurses Aides table for the Raritan Clinic East database by importing the data from a Microsoft Office Excel workbook.

1. Follow these steps to launch Get External Data:

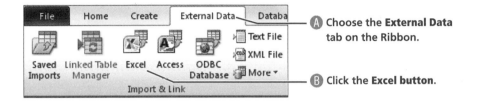

A Choose the **External Data** tab on the Ribbon.

B Click the **Excel button**.

Access launches the Get External Data – Excel Spreadsheet screen.

2. Follow these steps to locate the file to import:

A Click the **Browse** button in the Get External Data window.

B Navigate to the folder that contains your student data files and **double-click** the Nurses Aides.xlsx filename.

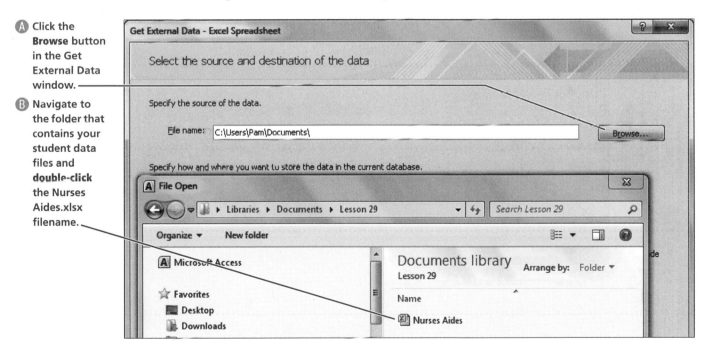

3. Select the **Import the Source Data into a New Table in the Current Database** option in the Get External Data window and click **OK**.
Access launches the Import Spreadsheet Wizard.

The workbook you are importing contains only one worksheet. As a result, Access skips the step asking you to select the worksheet containing the data to import. In future import actions, you will be prompted to select a worksheet when the workbook contains more than one worksheet.

4. Select the **First Row Contains Column Headings** checkbox and choose **Next**.
   The Wizard displays options for selecting the fields you want to import. For this practice, you will import all fields.

5. Choose **Next** to indicate that all fields in the worksheet should import to the new table.
   Access displays options for selecting or setting a key field.

6. Ensure that the **Let Access Add Primary Key** option is selected and then click **Next**.

7. Follow these steps to name and save the table:

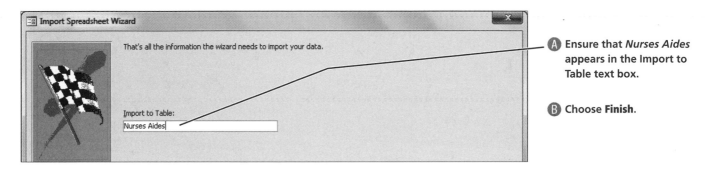

Ⓐ Ensure that *Nurses Aides* appears in the Import to Table text box.

Ⓑ Choose **Finish**.

8. Choose **Close** to close the Get External Data window.

View Data

9. Open the new **Nurses Aides** table to view the data.

10. **Close** the table and then **close** the database.

2.7 Creating a New Database Using a Template

Video Lesson labyrinthelab.com/videos

If you are familiar with Microsoft Word and Excel, you may also be familiar with templates. In Word, templates contain document format and design elements that help you create files that are consistent in their look and design.

Access also contains templates that enable you to create new databases—but in Access, a template is a ready-to-use database that contains all the tables, queries, forms, and reports needed to perform a specific task. When you need to create a database to track expenses or manage contacts, you can create the database using the appropriate template. After you create a database using a template, you can modify it to better meet your needs.

Access comes with a collection of sample templates that you can access from the File→New tab in Backstage view. In addition to accessing sample templates, you can use the Backstage view to access recently used templates and collections of templates found on the Microsoft website.

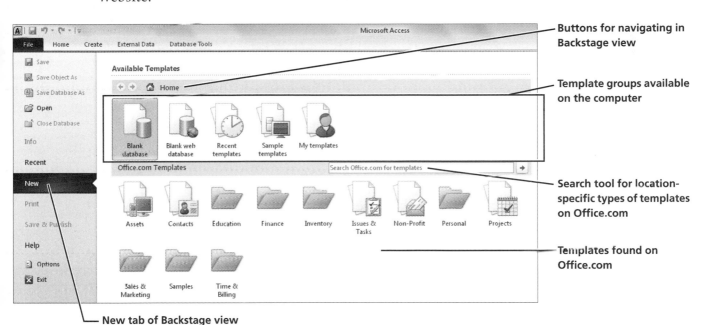

The categories of templates in each group may change as more templates become available.

QUICK REFERENCE	CREATING A DATABASE USING A TEMPLATE
Task	**Procedure**
Create a database using a template	▪ Display the Backstage view and select the New tab. ▪ Select the appropriate template group from the Available templates list or search for the template on Office.com. ▪ Click the template that corresponds to the database type you want to create. ▪ Click the Browse button and navigate to the folder in which you want to save the new database. ▪ Type a filename for the database in the File Name text box and click OK.

Create a Tasks Database

In this exercise, you will create a new database using the Tasks template.

1. **Launch** Access, if it is closed, and follow these steps to create a new database using a template:

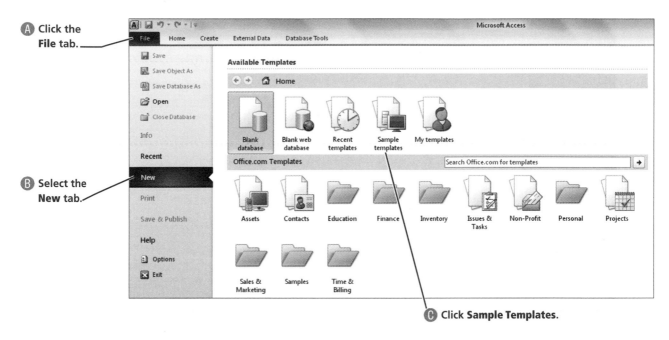

Ⓐ Click the **File** tab.

Ⓑ Select the **New** tab.

Ⓒ Click **Sample Templates.**

Access displays a list of sample databases in the Backstage view.

2. Follow these steps to select the database type and save the new database:

Ⓐ Click the **Tasks** database icon.

Ⓑ Type **Semester Tasks** in the File Name text box.

Ⓒ Click the **Browse** button, if necessary, to open the folder in which to store the database.

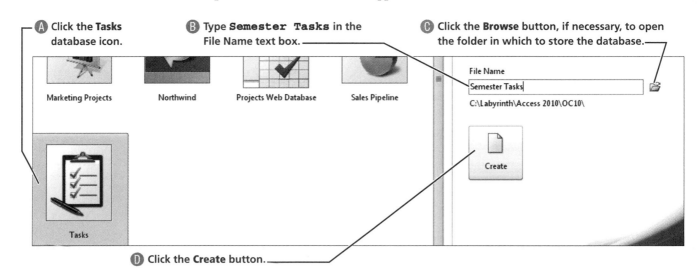

Ⓓ Click the **Create** button.

Access downloads the template, saves it using the filename you assigned, and then opens the database.

Review Database Objects

3. **Enable content**, if necessary, **open** the Navigation Pane, and then change the display in the Navigation Pane to display objects by **Object Type**.

4. **Open** each table, form, query, and report and review the arrangement of data in each object.

5. **Close** the database.

2.8 Managing Databases and Database Objects

Video Lesson labyrinthelab.com/videos

Documenting databases is an important step in the planning process for database files, and it makes up part of the managing process as well. Protecting databases and the data they contain as they grow is vital to the successful use of databases in any business. Ensuring that a minimum of data might be lost in the case of a natural disaster, power outage, and other normal occurrences will have managers throwing kudos your way! At the same time, learning efficient ways to manage database objects can save you a great deal of time as you build a database.

Saving Database Objects as New Objects

You most likely have already identified the value of using existing files as the basis for creating new files. For example, suppose you are sending out a number of letters that contain basically the same information. You can create the first letter, use the Save As command to save the letter as a new file, then edit the file to prevent having to retype the same paragraphs again.

Creating New Objects from Existing Objects

Often, databases contain different objects that are similar in structure and in the data they hold. For example, the Doctors table in your database for Raritan Clinic East contains fields similar to those fields found in the Nurses and Nurses Aides tables. When you are building a database that contains similar objects, you can copy the object, save it using a new object name, and then modify the new object to fit the specific data needs. Access provides two basic processes for copying objects:

■ Choose File→Save Object As. The default setting for the Save Object As command in Access opens the Save As dialog box and identifies the name of the new object being copied along with an object type.

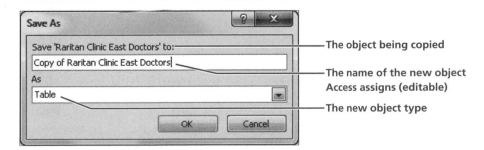

■ Right-click the object you want to copy and choose copy. Then, right-click the object area in the Navigation Pane and choose Paste.

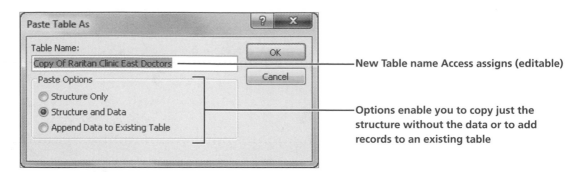

New Table name Access assigns (editable)

Options enable you to copy just the structure without the data or to add records to an existing table

QUICK REFERENCE	COPYING DATABASE OBJECTS
Task	**Procedure**
Copy a database object	■ Choose File→Save Object As.
	■ Type a name for the new object and click OK.
Copy a database table structure	■ In the Navigation Pane, right-click the table you want to copy.
	■ Select Copy and then right-click the Navigation Pane where you want to paste the new object.
	■ Select Paste and type a name for the new object in the Paste As dialog box.
	■ Select the Structure Only option in the Paste Options area.
	■ Click OK.
Save a database object as a new object	■ In the Navigation Pane, select the object you want to use as a basis for the new object.
	■ Choose File→Save Object As.
	■ Type a name for the new object in the Save As dialog box and click OK.

Save a Database Object as a New Object

In this exercise, you will save a database table in the Raritan Clinic East Employees database as a new table and edit the field names for the new table.

Before You Begin: The Raritan Clinic East Employees database should be open.

1. Select, but do **not** open, the **Raritan Clinic East Doctors** table.

2. Choose **File→Save Object As**.

3. Type **General Employees** in the Save 'Raritan Clinic East Doctors' To text box and click **OK**.

4. Click the **File** tab to close Backstage view; **open** the new General Employees table.

5. Choose **Home→Views→View** ![icon] on the Ribbon to switch to Design View.

6. Follow these steps to edit the field names for the General Employees table so that they appear as shown:

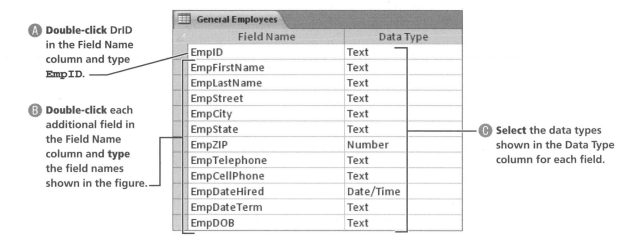

A **Double-click** DrID in the Field Name column and type **EmpID.**

B **Double-click** each additional field in the Field Name column and **type** the field names shown in the figure.

C **Select** the data types shown in the Data Type column for each field.

Access may present a warning message that records may be deleted because of the data type changes. For this exercise, it is okay to proceed.

7. **Save** 💾 changes to the General Employees table.

8. Choose **Design→Views→View** ▦ on the Ribbon to return to Datasheet View.

9. **Close** the table.

Backing Up a Database

Video Lesson   labyrinthelab.com/videos

Databases maintained by large corporations often have hundreds of thousands of records stored within. As a result, it is important to protect that data. Most companies have a backup procedure that they use to back up a network system including all files—not just databases—on a schedule. In addition to these safety procedures for protecting data, Access contains a backup feature you can use to back up your databases. It only takes a few minutes to keep hours of work safe!

When you back up a database using Access tools, Access places the date of the backup in the filename so that you can easily identify each backup file. You choose the drive and folder in which you want to save the backup.

QUICK REFERENCE	BACKING UP AND REPAIRING DATABASES
Task	**Procedure**
Back up a database	▪ Close all open database objects.
	▪ File→Save & Publish→Back Up Database.
	▪ Navigate to the folder in which you want to save the backup.
	▪ Choose Save.

Back Up a Database

In this exercise, you will back up your Raritan Clinic East Employees database.

Before You Begin: The Raritan Clinic East Employees database should be open.

1. **Close** all open objects in your Raritan Clinic East Employees database.

2. Choose **File→Save & Publish→Save Database As→Back Up Database** and then click the Save As button.

   Access displays the Save As dialog box and places the date at the end of the database filename.

3. Navigate to the Lesson 02 folder, and then click **Save** to save the backup using the default filename Access assigned.

   Access saves the new backup file to the desired location; however, the database file "in use" is still the original Raritan Clinic East Employees database. This is different from, say, using Save As with a Word Document, in which the renamed file becomes the one in use.

2.9 Concepts Review

| Concepts Review | labyrinthelab.com/acc10 |

To check your knowledge of the key concepts introduced in this lesson, complete the Concepts Review quiz by going to the URL listed above. If your classroom is using Labyrinth eLab, you may complete the Concepts Review quiz from within your eLab course.

Reinforce Your Skills

Create a Table Using Design View

First Perk has worked diligently to implement some of the database features recommended by their consulting team. In this exercise, you will help them build additional objects in their database.

1. Launch **Access** and **open** the rs-First Perk Objects database from the Lesson 02 folder.

2. **Save** the database using the filename **rs-First Perk Objects Rev**.

3. Choose **Create→Tables→Table** on the Ribbon to create a new table.

4. Choose **Datasheet→Views→View** ☑ on the Ribbon to switch to Design View.

5. Type **Coffee Types** in the Table Name text box and click **OK** to save the table.

6. Select **ID** in the first field and type **Category Number** to replace ID.

7. **Press** [Tab], **click** the Data Type list button, and select **Text**.

8. **Press** [Tab] and **type** the following in the Description column:
   Single Letter representing category type C, D, F; 1-digit Strength; 2-digit Origin; 2-digit Number.

9. Complete the following list of fields, data types, and descriptions for the table:

Field Name	Data Type	Description
Coffee Name	Text	
Category Type	Text	Caffeinated, Decaffeinated, Free Trade.
Strength	Text	Regular, Espresso, Flavored, Special, Light.
Country of Origin	Text	
Description	Text	

10. **Save** 🖫 changes to the table and **close** ☒ it.

Append Records to a Table

Now that you have the structure for the Coffee Types table completed, you can import records into the table and append them so that you have a complete a list of First Perk coffees. In this exercise, you will import the list of currently available coffee from an Excel worksheet and append the data to the table.

Before You Begin: The rs-First Perk Objects Rev database should be open.

1. **Select** the Coffee Types table, and then choose **External Data→Import & Link→Excel** on the Ribbon to launch the Get External Data dialog box.

2. Click the **Browse** button at the right end of the Filename text box, **navigate** to the Lesson 02 folder, and **double-click** the rs-First Perk Coffees.xls file to open it.

3. **Select** the Append a Copy of the Records to the Table option and confirm that the Coffee Types table appears in the table name text box.

4. Click **OK** to launch the Import Spreadsheet Wizard.

5. **Select** the following settings in each of the Wizard screens, clicking Next to advance to the next screen.

   - Screen 1: Show Worksheets: Sheet 1.
   - Screen 2: First Row Contains Column Headings.
   - Screen 3: Import to Table Coffee Types.

6. Click **Finish**, and then click **Close**.

7. **Open** the Coffee Types table and review the data.

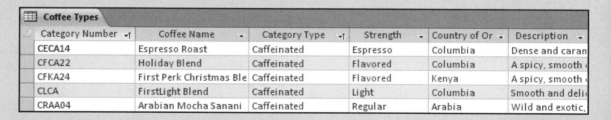

8. **Close** ☒ the table. **Save** changes when prompted.

Create a Form and a Report

The First Perk database is taking shape. In this exercise, you will add a form and a report to the database.

1. Launch **Access** and **open** the rs-First Perk Objects Rev database if it is closed.

2. Select the **Menu Items** table and choose **Create→Forms→Form** on the Ribbon to create a form for the table.

3. **Save** the form using the form name **Menu Items**.

4. Select the **Menu Items** table again and choose **Create→Reports→Report** on the Ribbon.

5. **Save** the report using the report name **Menu Items**.

6. **Close** the form and report.

Import a Table

The First Perk database currently contains two tables. In preparation for opening the business, the owners stored data about the people they have hired in an Excel worksheet. In this exercise, you will import the data from the worksheet to create a new table for the database.

1. **Launch** Access and open the rs-First Perk Objects Rev database if it is closed.

2. Choose **External Data→Import & Link→Excel** on the Ribbon to launch the Get External Data window.

3. Choose **Browse** and navigate to the folder that contains your student data files.

4. **Double-click** the rs-First Perk Employees.xls workbook, **select** the Import the Source Data into a New Table in the Current Database option, and click **OK** to launch the Import Spreadsheet Wizard.

5. Select the **Show Worksheets** option, select **Sheet1**, and choose **Next**.

6. **Check** the First Row Contains Column Headings checkbox and choose **Next**.

7. Choose **Next** to let Access know you want to import all the data.

8. Select the **Let Access Add Primary Key** option and choose **Next**.

9. Type **First Perk Workers** in the Import to Table text box, choose **Finish**, and then choose **Close** to close the Get External Data window.

10. Display **All Access Objects by Object Type** in the Navigation Pane, **open** the First Perk Workers table and **review** the data.

Apply Your Skills

Create a New Database Using a Template

Several of the sample templates available in Access are designed to store data related to education such as Students and Faculty, class lists, and so forth. In this exercise, you will use the Education templates to create a new database designed to store student data.

1. Launch **Access** and display the **sample templates**.

2. Create a **new** database using the Students template, name the database **as-NSW Students-xxx** where xxx represents your initials, and **save** the file in the folder in which you are storing your student files.

3. **Close** the Student List form that opens when you create the database, **enable content**, and then **open** the Navigation Pane.

4. **Group** objects on the Navigation Pane by **Object Type** and review the tables Access created. Answer the following questions:

   ■ What tables are you surprised to see separated from larger, more complex, tables?

   ■ What fields of data are included in database tables that you would have forgotten to include if you had created the database?

   ■ What forms and reports are shown in the database that might also be included in other databases?

5. **Add** your name and other data (real or fictional) to the **Student List** form in the database.

6. **Close** the form, but leave the database **open** for the next exercise.

Import Students into the Database

A preliminary list of students appears in a worksheet named as-NSW Students.xls. In this exercise, you will import the data into a new table in your as-NSW Students-xxx database.

1. **Open** your as-NSW Students-xxx database if it is closed.

2. Import all data in **Sheet1** of the as-NSW Students.xls file. The first row of the worksheet contains field names and there is no primary key field.

3. **Save** the table using the table name **NSW Students**.

4. **Open** the Navigation Pane, arrange the database objects by Students Navigation, and locate the group of unassigned objects.

5. **Open** all objects in this group, study the data, **open** the as-NSW Students.xlsx workbook file in Excel, and then answer these questions:

   ■ How many objects did Access create when you imported the worksheet?

   ■ Did one of the objects have "Error" in the object title?

   ■ What does the object containing the word "Error" have in it? Do you know why?

6. **Enter** fictitious data into the record from the Excel file that caused the error, and then **delete** the error object from the database.

7. **Close** the database and **exit** Access.

Create Objects

In this lesson, you learned that you can import data from Excel files and use the data to create tables in Access. You can also import data from other databases and append the data to existing tables or use the tables to create new tables in the database.

The VonHamburg Tomb database currently contains one table. Other tables were added to the wrong database and need to be imported from that database into the VonHamburg Tomb database. In this exercise, you will import the tables from the database.

1. **Open** the as-VonHamburg Tomb database and save the database using the filename **as-VonHamburg Tomb-xxx**, substituting your initials for the xxx.

2. Using the External Data tools, **import** the Access database named as-Antiques so you can import a table from this database.

3. Choose the **Tables** tab to make it active and then choose **Select All** and click **OK** to import all five tables into the as-VonHamburg Tomb-xxx database.

4. **Open** and examine each table.

5. **Create** a form for each table except the Selling Format table, **saving** the form using the table name.

6. **Create** a report for the Records table.

7. **Print** a copy of the Records report.

8. **Close** all open objects, **close** the database, and **exit** Access.

Create a New Database with Objects

The Slaughter Dental Clinic has just purchased Microsoft Office. They would like for you to create a new database to hold patient information. In this exercise, you will use the list of fields created for the doctors and nurses at Raritan Clinic East to create a table to hold patient data.

1. **Launch** Access, **create** a new blank database, and **save** the database using the filename **as-Slaughter Dental Clinic-xx**, substituting your initials for the xx.

2. **Add** fields to Table1 using the fields you identified as required for patients.

3. **Save** the table using the table name **Clinic Patients**.

4. **Create** a form named **Clinic Patients** for entering data into the patients table.

5. **Enter** your personal (or fictional) data to the database and **print** a copy of your data as a form.

6. **Close** the database and **exit** Access.

Critical Thinking & Work-Readiness Skills

In the course of working through the following Microsoft Office-based Critical Thinking exercises, you will also be utilizing various work-readiness skills, some of which are listed next to each exercise. Go to labyrinthelab.com/ workreadiness to learn more about the work-readiness skills.

2.1 Locate a Template and Build a Database

Customer service representatives in the accounting department at Raritan Clinic East have asked James Elliott to create a database for logging customer calls. To help James, search the web for two database templates designed for customer service use and follow onscreen instructions for downloading. Then, create a new database using each template and review the tables, forms, and reports. Save the databases in your Lesson 02 folder as **ct-Customer Service1** and **ct-Customer Service2**. If working in a group, discuss similarities and differences among the templates as well as which template, in general, would best help customer service reps log customer calls. If working alone, type your response in a Word document named **ct-Questions** saved to your Lesson 02 folder.

WORK-READINESS SKILLS APPLIED

- Serving clients/ customers
- Applying technology to a task
- Participating as a member of a team

2.2 Import Tables from One Database to Another

Service Guild at Raritan Clinic East would like to include information about donations from businesses and ticket sales for the home tour in the ct-Service Guild Membership database (Lesson 02 folder). A database used by another organization to record donations and pledges has been located. Review and incorporate the tables that might be used by Service Guild for recording donations, pledges, and names and addresses. Open ct-Charitable Contributions from your Lesson 02 folder. Review the tables, forms, and reports and determine which tables would work well for Service Guild. Save the ct-Service Guild Membership database as **ct-Service Guild Revised** and import the appropriate tables into it. Create and name simple forms and reports for the new tables you import.

WORK-READINESS SKILLS APPLIED

- Improving or designing systems
- Reasoning
- Making decisions

2.3 Create a Database with Excel Data

Raritan Clinic East, to encourage the use of local natural resources, is designing floral arrangements in the gift shop using native, natural wildflowers to help build a Green Scene. Create a database named **ct-Flowers in [Your State]** in your Lesson 02 folder. Import the list of flowers found in ct-Flowers.xlsx (Lesson 02 folder) into a new table named **Flowers**. From the table, create a form and a report. Then, search the Internet (or contact a local plant nursery) to learn what flowers in the table would grow well in your state. Add a State field to the Flowers table, formatting it as a Yes/No field. Check at least five flowers you know will grow well in your state. Print copies of the table, form, and report.

WORK-READINESS SKILLS APPLIED

- Acquiring and evaluating information
- Thinking creatively
- Using computers to process information

Maintaining a Database

LESSON OUTLINE

3.1   Formatting a Table Datasheet Layout

3.2   Modifying Table Structures

3.3   Setting Lookup Fields Using the Lookup Wizard

3.4   Setting Field Properties

3.5   Retrieving Data

3.6   Previewing and Printing Data

3.7   Concepts Review

Reinforce Your Skills

Apply Your Skills

Critical Thinking & Work-Readiness Skills

LEARNING OBJECTIVES

After studying this lesson, you will be able to:

- Change the layout of a table by adjusting column width, hiding columns, and rearranging column layout
- Locate and update records by sorting, filtering, and using Find and Replace
- Enhance a datasheet
- Set table field properties
- Rename, copy, and delete database objects

Most databases are designed and set up by professionals who are database experts. As a result, most company employees are simply required to maintain databases—a task that most people are already accustomed to doing. Consider, for example, the address book you use to store addresses of friends and relatives. Each time someone listed in the address book moves or changes phone numbers, you edit the information in your address book.

The same concept is true of electronic databases. Employees come and go, patients relocate to new addresses, phone numbers change, and websites come online. Updating database data to reflect these changes helps maintain the usefulness of the data. In this lesson, you will learn how to adjust the layout of columns in a datasheet, modify data field properties to control and display data more consistently, change the name of a database table, locate and retrieve data from a database for editing or removal, and copy and delete objects in a database.

Cleaning Up and Standardizing Data

As James Elliott continues his work in the human resources department at Raritan Clinic East, other employees and administrators are beginning to request that he locate information from the database he is building. As he reviews and locates the information, he realizes that the format of data is mixed—some data is entered in all capital letters while other data is in mixed case. In addition, the format of telephone numbers and other items appears unformatted in the database, and some datasheet columns are too narrow to display the information appropriately. It is now time for James to clean up and format the data.

Raritan Clinic East

Pediatric Diagnostic Specialists

The awkward field names could better identify the data in each column.

The column headings and some of the data are truncated—cut off because of the narrow columns.

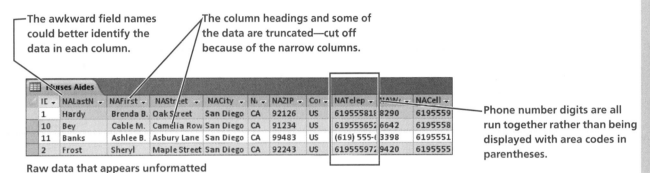

Phone number digits are all run together rather than being displayed with area codes in parentheses.

Raw data that appears unformatted

The ID number identifies the employee position.

Column headings are more meaningful.

Data displays fully in each column.

Phone numbers are formatted properly.

Raw data entered and formatted using property settings

Video Lesson labyrinthelab.com/videos

Two tasks frequently associated with databases include adding records to database tables and formatting the layout of the datasheet to display field data. In many cases, these are two primary tasks of data entry personnel. By now, you already know how to add records to a table, so this section will focus on formatting the datasheet layout.

Several of the columns in the Nurses Aides table are so narrow that the data in the columns appears to be cut off. The data in narrow columns is still there—Access displays only the portion of the data that fits within the column width and *truncates* (stores without displaying) the additional data. You can maximize the Access window to provide more space for the table and close the Navigation Pane to provide even more space for objects you have open. These actions simply allow more columns of data to appear onscreen without affecting the width of each column.

Changing the Width of Columns

You can adjust the width of each column in a datasheet to display all data in the column. Access gives you some useful techniques for changing column width.

- **Drag a column border**—Dragging a column border enables you to make the column on the left of the border wider or narrower.

- **Double-click a column heading border**—Double-clicking a right border of a column changes the width of the column on the left to fit the longest data entry in the column or the column heading, whichever is wider.

- **Right-click field heading and choose Field Width**—Selecting the Field Width command from the context menu opens the Column Width dialog box so you can type the appropriate column width, reset the standard column width, or select Best Fit to automatically size the field width to the longest entry.

The data in these columns is truncated because the column widths are too narrow.

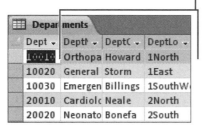

Widening the column widths prevents truncation.

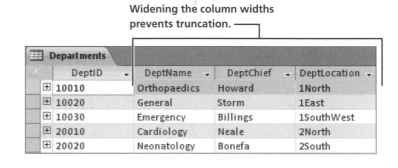

Moving and Hiding Data Columns

In addition, there will be times when you want to reposition a column of data in a table layout or hide some columns so that you can view other field columns. Access contains tools that enable you to rearrange columns and hide columns. When you rearrange the columns in a datasheet, the fields in the table layout remain in their original positions but are simply displayed in a different order in the datasheet. When you hide columns, Access temporarily removes them from display. The data, however, remains in the table—it is NOT deleted. When you want to view data in hidden columns, you can unhide the column.

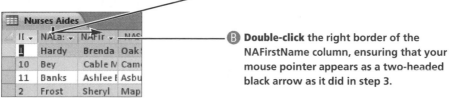

Before and after hiding the E-mail Address column.

Saving a Table Layout

Changing the layout of a table datasheet has no real effect on table data or table structure; however, when you make changes to a table datasheet, Access recognizes the differences between the layout and the structure of the table and prompts you to save the changes to the layout when you close the table. If you abandon the changes you make to the layout, the next time you open the table datasheet, the column widths will return to their original size, the hidden columns will show, and the repositioned columns will occupy their original place in the layout. If you save the changes, the next time you open the table datasheet, Access recalls the layout and displays the datasheet as you formatted it.

FROM THE KEYBOARD

Ctrl+S to save changes to the table layout

The shape and color of the mouse pointer is important when you are adjusting column width and repositioning columns in a table or datasheet layout. Be sure to pay attention to the mouse pointer shape as you work.

DEVELOP YOUR SKILLS 3.1.1
Format a Table Datasheet Layout

In this exercise, you will adjust the column widths of table datasheet columns, hide columns, and reposition columns.

1. **Open** the Raritan Clinic East Employees database from the Lesson 3 folder and **save** a copy of the database as **Raritan Clinic East–Formatted**, enabling content if prompted.

2. **Display** the Navigation Pane and **open** the Nurses Aides table.

3. Follow these steps to change the width of the first table column:

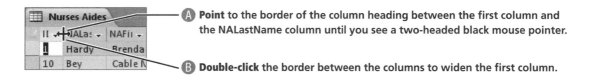

Ⓐ **Point** to the border of the column heading between the first column and the NALastName column until you see a two-headed black mouse pointer.

Ⓑ **Double-click** the border between the columns to widen the first column.

4. Follow these steps to change the width of two columns at the same time:

Ⓐ **Point** to the column heading NALastName, ensuring that you see a black down-pointing arrow, **click and drag** the pointer to the right toward NAFirstName to select both columns.

Ⓑ **Double-click** the right border of the NAFirstName column, ensuring that your mouse pointer appears as a two-headed black arrow as it did in step 3.

5. Follow these steps to reposition the NAWorkExtension column:

Ⓐ **Click** the NAWorkExtension column heading to select the column.

Ⓑ **Point** to the selected NAWorkExtension column heading, ensuring that the mouse pointer appears **as a white arrow**.

Ⓒ **Drag** the NAWorkExtension column heading to a position to the right of the NACell field. As you drag the column, a black vertical bar indicates the active position of the column. If you drop the column before it is properly placed, point to the column heading and drag it to the proper position.

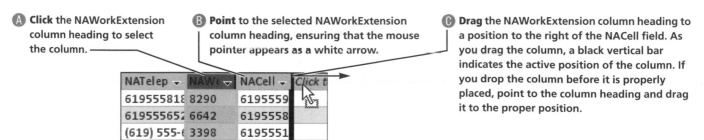

6. Follow these steps to hide the Country column:

Ⓐ **Right-click** the Country column heading to display the shortcut menu.

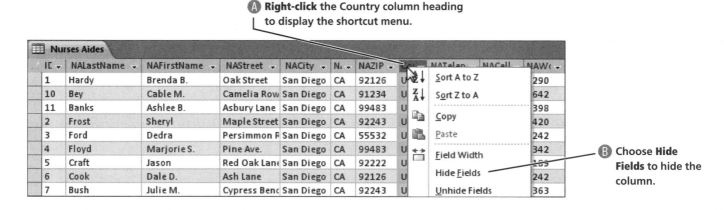

Ⓑ Choose **Hide Fields** to hide the column.

7. Follow these steps to redisplay the Country column and hide the Click to Add field:

Ⓐ **Right-click** any column heading and choose Unhide Fields.

Ⓑ Click the **Country** field checkbox to check it and unhide the column.

Ⓒ Click the **Click to Add** field checkbox to clear the checkmark—clearing the checkbox hides it.

Ⓓ Click **Close**.

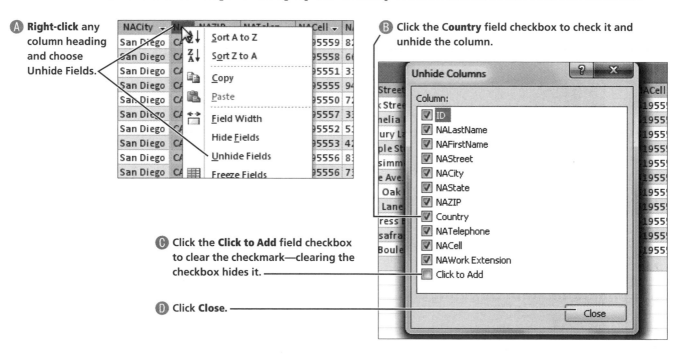

8. Click the **Save** 💾 button to save changes to the table layout.

9. **Close** ✕ the table.

Enhancing a Datasheet

Video Lesson   labyrinthelab.com/videos

Changing the datasheet layout enables you to make the necessary adjustments to the datasheet so that you can view complete field data and change field arrangement when necessary. Enhancing the datasheet layout enables you to display data in a more attractive or aesthetically pleasing format. Some of the features you can change by enhancing the datasheet include:

- The appearance of gridlines
- The font, font size, and font color
- The table background color

As you apply enhancements to the datasheet, Access formats all data and gridlines to match the format you choose.

Formatting the Datasheet Using the Ribbon

Two distinct Ribbon tabs contain tools for enhancing a datasheet:

- The Home tab displays tools for enhancing the most commonly formatted features on a datasheet such as font, gridlines, color, fill, and alignment.

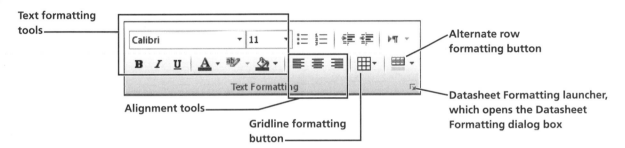

Text formatting tools

Alternate row formatting button

Datasheet Formatting launcher, which opens the Datasheet Formatting dialog box

Alignment tools

Gridline formatting button

- The Table Tools→Fields tab contains tools for setting the data type and data format for numeric and currency data.

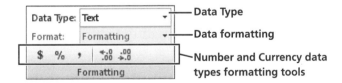

Data Type

Data formatting

Number and Currency data types formatting tools

In addition to the Ribbon tools, the Datasheet Formatting dialog box contains tools that enable you to change the background color of table cells as well as the line style for the table.

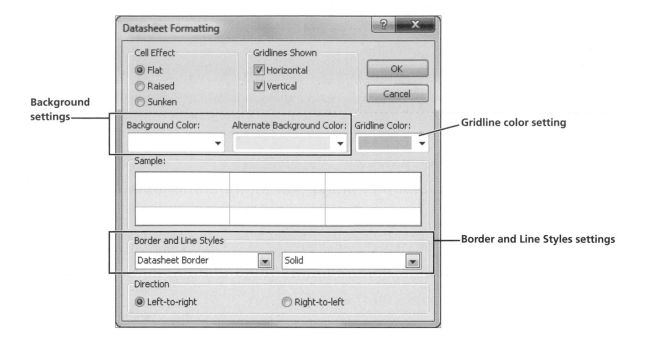

Background settings

Gridline color setting

Border and Line Styles settings

Enhance a Datasheet

In this exercise, you will use the Home tab to set datasheet enhancement options for the Departments table in the Raritan Clinic East—Formatted database.

Format Background for Alternate Rows

1. Open the **Departments** table in the Raritan Clinic East—Formatted database.
   The DeptID for the first record is active.

2. Choose **Home→Text Formatting→Alternate Row Color menu arrow** to display the palette of colors.

3. Click the **Blue, Accent 1** color button on the top row of the palette.

Format Datasheet Font

4. Choose **Home→Text Formatting→Font drop-down list arrow** Arial and select the **Arial** font.

Format Gridlines

5. Choose **Home→Text Formatting→Gridlines drop-down list arrow** and select **Gridlines: Horizontal** from the Gridlines menu.

6. Click the **Home→Text Formatting→Datasheet Formatting** dialog box launcher on the Ribbon to open the Datasheet Formatting dialog box.

7. Follow these steps to change the gridline color:

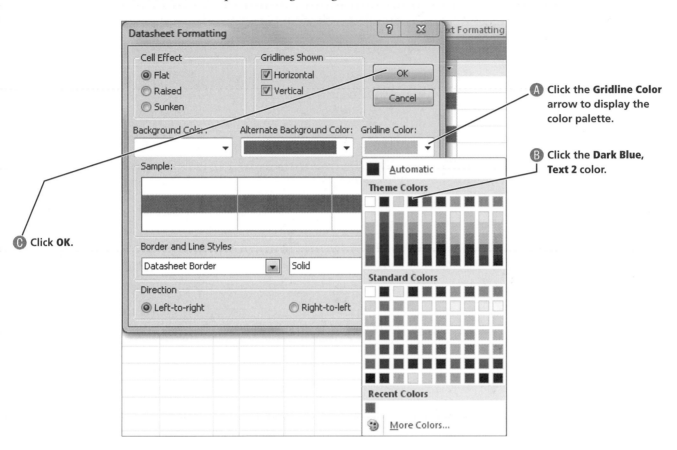

Ⓐ Click the **Gridline Color** arrow to display the color palette.

Ⓑ Click the **Dark Blue, Text 2** color.

Ⓒ Click **OK**.

8. Save changes to the table and then **close** it.

3.2 Modifying Table Structures

Video Lesson labyrinthelab.com/videos

The integrity of a database and the validity of data are important aspects of database maintenance. Access offers a number of features that enable you to modify table fields, control the data entered, and format the data to ensure consistent reporting. These features include, but are not limited to:

- Renaming tables, forms, and other database objects
- Adding and removing fields from tables
- Arranging the position of fields within the underlying table structure
- Setting properties to control the values that data entry personnel can enter into the fields

Renaming Tables and Editing, Adding, and Deleting Table Fields

As you create tables in an Access database, you define each field by setting the data type and entering the field name. Access works behind the scenes and sets properties for the field that control the number of characters the field can contain as well as the format of the data and the type of characters that are valid for the field data. You can accept the default properties Access sets or modify the properties. Properties available depend on the data type selected for the field. Modifying database tables by adding, editing, or deleting fields should be approached with care because of the impact such actions would have on the table data.

Renaming Tables

When you save a database table, you give the table a name that identifies, in general, the data that the table contains. You can change the name of a table without affecting the data it holds. As you progress in your study of Access, however, you will start to realize that table names are often included in other database objects that use the data they contain. As a result, renaming a table can have a trickle-down effect on other database objects.

Adding Fields to Existing Tables

Periodically, you will need to create new fields in existing database tables, and then add data to these fields. You can add a field either in Datasheet View or in Table Design View, and then position the field in the layout where you want it to appear.

Deleting Fields

When you delete a field that contains data, Access displays a message warning you that deleting the field removes all data from the field. If you delete a field by mistake in Design view and have not yet saved the table structure, you can recover the deleted field using the Undo command. If, however, you save the table after deleting the field, the data is lost and you have to add the field to the Table Design and then re-enter all field data in the table to restore the data. When the warning message appears and you choose Yes, Access removes the field and the field row in the upper pane of Design View or the column in Datasheet View remains active.

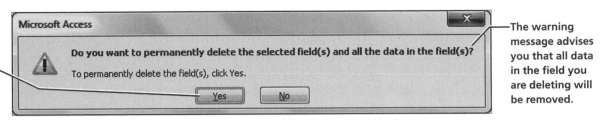

The selected field will be deleted if you choose Yes.

The warning message advises you that all data in the field you are deleting will be removed.

Take great care whenever you decide to delete a field from a table. It could take many hours of hard work to re-create it.

Editing Field Data Types

Each Data Type available in Access starts with a different letter. As a result, you can type the first letter of a valid data type and the data type that begins with that letter will display. For example, if you want to change the Data Type from Text to Date/Time, you can move to the Data Type column for the field and type D. Access changes the Data Type value to Date/Time. Anytime you change a data type for a field that contains values that fail to conform to the new data type, Access deletes the field data for nonconforming records. For example, if you change a Text data type field to a Date/Time data type and some of the data in the field has been formatted using hyphens in the date, as in 6-21-75, Access will warn you that you are about to delete data. At that point, you can determine whether or not you want to continue.

Using the Yes/No Data Type

The Yes/No field data type sets the field so that only two entries are possible. These entries can be Yes/No, True/False, On/Off, or any number of additional combinations of alternate single-character entries that you might want to place in a field. When you set the Yes/No data type for a field, Access places a checkbox for the field in the datasheet and on forms where the data appears. Checking the checkbox indicates a value of Yes, True, On, etc.; clearing the checkbox indicates a value of No, False, or Off.

FROM THE KEYBOARD
Spacebar to check and uncheck a checkbox

Quantity in Stock	Reorder Level	Order
20	25	☑
10	5	☐
8	10	☑
5	15	☑

Checkmarks identify products that should be ordered.

DEVELOP YOUR SKILLS 3.2.1
Modify the Table Structure

In this exercise, you will rename the Raritan Clinic East Doctors table, delete a field from the table, add a field to the table, and modify the data type for a field. The Raritan Clinic East—Formatted database should be open when you start this exercise.

1. **Right-click** the Raritan Clinic East Doctors table and choose **Rename**.

2. Type **Doctors** and **press** Enter.

3. **Right-click** the Doctors table in the Navigation Pane and select **Design View**.

4. Follow these steps to delete a field from the table:

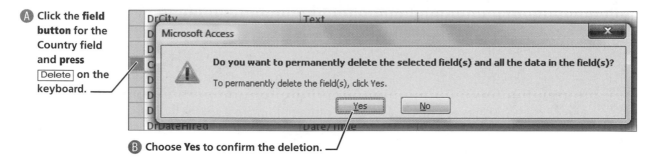

Ⓐ Click the **field button** for the Country field and press Delete on the keyboard.

Ⓑ Choose **Yes** to confirm the deletion.

Access deletes the field and moves remaining fields up the field list.

Add New Fields

5. Follow these steps to add a new field to the Doctors table:

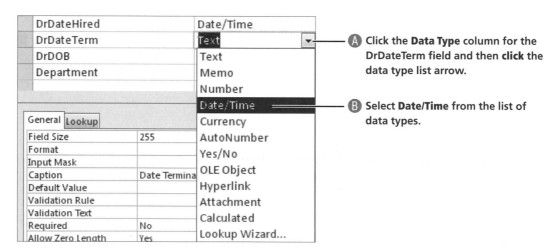

Ⓐ **Right-click** the DrTelephone field row button and select **Insert Rows**.

Ⓑ Type **DrWorkExtension** in the Field Name column.

Ⓒ **Press** Tab and set the Data Type to **Text**.

6. Add a new field named **Department** to the bottom of the field list.

7. Follow these steps to change the data type for a field:

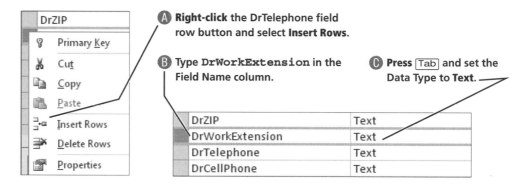

Ⓐ Click the **Data Type** column for the DrDateTerm field and then **click** the data type list arrow.

Ⓑ Select **Date/Time** from the list of data types.

8. Repeat the procedures identified in **step 7** to change the DrDOB field data type to **Date/Time**.

9. **Save** changes to the table and then choose **Home→Views→View→Datasheet** to switch back to Datasheet view.

10. Follow these steps to expand all columns of the Doctors table datasheet at the same time:

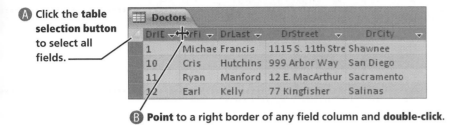

Ⓐ Click the **table selection button** to select all fields.

Ⓑ **Point** to a right border of any field column and **double-click.**

11. **Add** the last four digits of your telephone number to the DrWorkExtension field for Dr. Michael Francis in the table.

12. **Close** the table, **saving** changes when prompted.

3.3 Setting Lookup Fields Using the Lookup Wizard

Video Lesson   labyrinthelab.com/videos

All tables in a database are related in some way to each other as well as to other objects in the database. Database forms, reports, and queries use the data contained in tables when you display them. In some cases, data from one table is also used in another table to connect or relate the two tables.

For example, if you wanted to identify the clinic department number in which each doctor or nurse worked, you would normally enter the data by typing it into the Doctors or Nurses table. Because many clinics have numerous departments, each identified by a unique department number, it is possible that data entry clerks could refer to a department by an unofficial number or name. Such actions would result in errors in the data that would be compounded as your database grows.

To ensure that the data entered into each table field is valid, Access provides a field data type known as a *lookup field*. A lookup field enables you to select a field value in one table by looking up values from another table or from a list of values entered by the database designer. The list of valid entries appears in a drop-down list in the table using the values.

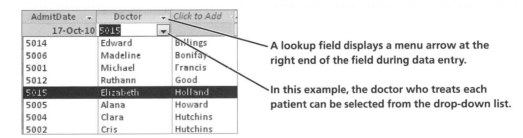

A lookup field displays a menu arrow at the right end of the field during data entry.

In this example, the doctor who treats each patient can be selected from the drop-down list.

Using a lookup value also enables you to look up values from one field and return a value from a different field in the connected table. For example, you can look up a department number by typing the common department name that you do know, and Access will display that department number.

Examining the Benefits of Lookup Tables

Adding a lookup field to a table serves three primary purposes:

- It reduces the time required to enter the data repeatedly.
- It reduces errors associated with data entry.
- It restricts data to valid entries.

For example, if you are processing time card data before issuing employee checks, setting a lookup field of valid employee IDs helps ensure that only valid employees receive checks. Lookup fields also help reduce the number of redundant fields contained in database tables.

Performing a Lookup

Access provides the following two ways to use the Lookup feature:

- **Lookup Wizard**—A data type that launches the Lookup Wizard, which walks you through the process of setting up a lookup field.

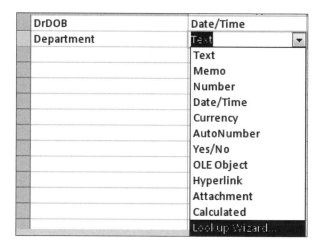

The Lookup Wizard data type.

- **Lookup tab**—An option in the Field Properties pane that sets the data source containing the values you want to display in the field.

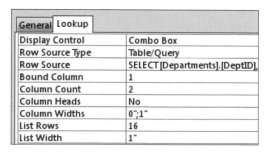

The Lookup tab in the Field Properties pane of the Table Design View.

Using the Lookup Wizard is a good way to learn how the settings for a lookup field are determined.

Set a Lookup Field Using a Wizard

In this exercise, you will use the Lookup Wizard to create a lookup field in the Doctors table that displays a list of valid departments. You will then use the lookup field to enter data into the Doctors table. The Raritan Clinic East—Formatted database should be open.

1. Display the **Doctors** table in Design View.

2. Follow these steps to launch the Lookup Wizard:

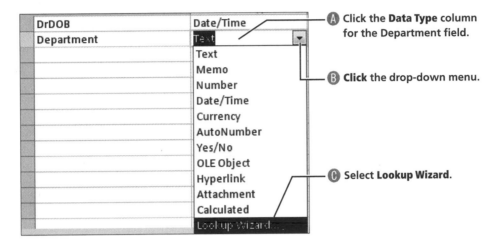

Ⓐ Click the **Data Type** column for the Department field.

Ⓑ **Click** the drop-down menu.

Ⓒ Select **Lookup Wizard**.

Access displays the first screen of the Lookup Wizard.

3. Choose the **I Want the Lookup Column to Get the Values from Another Table or Query** option, and then click **Next**.
   The Wizard asks you to identify the table containing the values to look up.

4. Follow these steps to identify the table containing the values to look up:

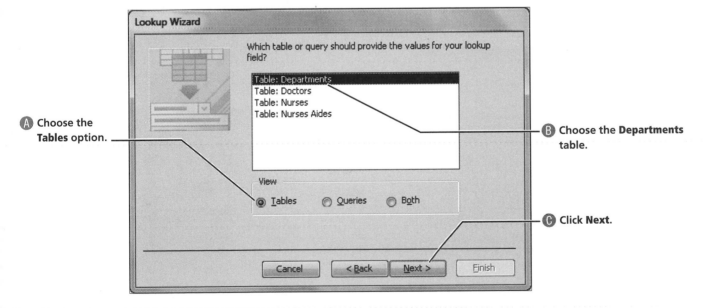

Ⓐ Choose the **Tables** option.

Ⓑ Choose the **Departments** table.

Ⓒ Click **Next**.

5. Follow these steps to set up the fields containing values Access should examine:

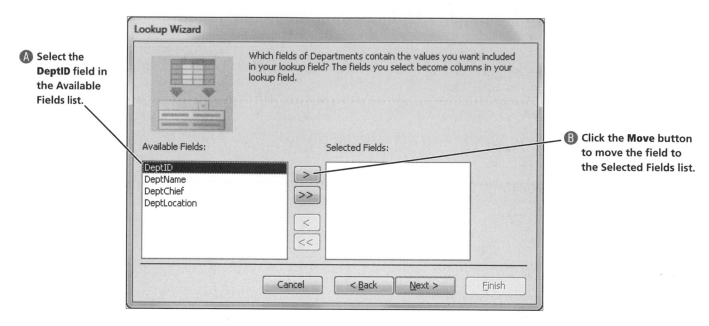

Ⓐ Select the **DeptID** field in the Available Fields list.

Ⓑ Click the **Move** button to move the field to the Selected Fields list.

6. Repeat the procedures identified in **step 5** to move the DeptName field to the Selected Fields list and then click **Next**.

7. Follow these steps to set a sort field:

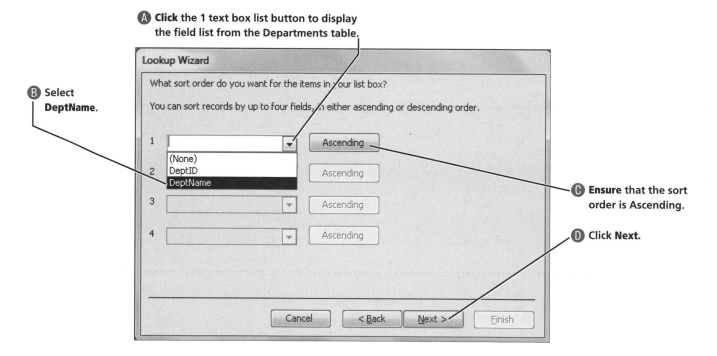

Ⓐ **Click** the 1 text box list button to display the field list from the Departments table.

Ⓑ **Select DeptName**.

Ⓒ **Ensure** that the sort order is Ascending.

Ⓓ **Click Next**.

8. Uncheck the **Hide Key Column** checkbox.

9. Click **Next**, select DeptID as the value to display when you select the Department, and then click **Finish**.
Access prompts you to save the table.

10. Choose **Yes** to save changes to the table.

Test the Lookup Field

11. Choose **Design→Views→View** ▦ on the Ribbon to display the datasheet.

12. Follow these steps to review the lookup field format:

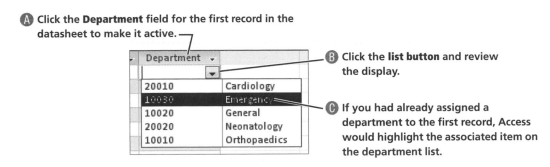

Ⓐ Click the **Department** field for the first record in the datasheet to make it active.

Ⓑ Click the **list button** and review the display.

Ⓒ If you had already assigned a department to the first record, Access would highlight the associated item on the department list.

Department ▾	
20010	Cardiology
10030	Emergency
10020	General
20020	Neonatology
10010	Orthopaedics

If you were entering new records, you could display the drop-down list and select the name of the department. Access would place the number associated with the department in the table.

13. **Close** ☒ the table. Choose **Yes** if prompted to save any changes.

3.4 Setting Field Properties

Video Lesson <u>labyrinthelab.com/videos</u>

Field properties are settings that enable you to control the characteristics of each field. The Field Properties pane appears in the lower portion of the Table Design View. You can set and define multiple properties for each field in the table. In addition, setting features such as a primary key or data type controls, to some extent, the settings Access applies to fields. The most frequently used properties are identified in the following table.

QUICK REFERENCE	IDENTIFYING COMMON FIELD PROPERTIES
Field Property	**Description**
Field Size	Sets a field length that controls the number of data characters each field can hold.
Caption	Sets a column heading title that describes the data content better than the actual field name.
Input Mask	Identifies the format of values entered—alphabetic or numeric, uppercase or lowercase, with hyphens or without, etc.
Validation Rule	Controls actual values entered into fields—less than 100, greater than 1000, like Dr-.
Validation Text	Provides a tip that identifies valid data entries.
Default Value	Adds a default value for a specific field in each record.

Why Set Field Properties?

Different people frequently add data to a database—and they often enter the data differently. Take, for example, phone numbers. Some people type parentheses around the area code when they enter phone numbers so that the data appears (970) 555-2975. Other people separate the area code from the number using a hyphen, creating a phone number that resembles 970-555-2975. Both formats for the data are correct and both are accurate; however, when you display mismatched data formats in a report, they can be distracting. Entering parentheses or hyphens as you type data into tables can also be time consuming. Setting field properties that control how data appears helps maintain data consistency throughout the database tables that filters down to ensure that the data appears consistent in forms and reports.

Setting Field Size

The Field Size property limits the number of characters that can be entered into the field for each record. Field size is, perhaps, the most commonly set field property. For example, if you want to limit data entry of state names into a database table, you can set the State field size to two—forcing data entry to the two-character state abbreviation. Sometimes, when you reduce the field size to limit data entry, Access displays a message advising you that data may be lost. For example, if you change the field size for a State field from 255 characters to 2, Access tells you that data may be lost due to the reduced field size and asks if you want to continue. In most cases, you are familiar with the data that each record contains, so you can choose Yes. If you are uncertain whether data entered for all records meets the new field size limitation, you may want to choose No, check the data to ensure that it fits the new limit, and then set the field size.

Setting Captions

The Caption field property enables you to type an alternate name for a field so it appears more appropriately on forms, in datasheets, and on reports. As you may have noticed, many field names contain no spaces or include an underscore, such as in Field_Name, to identify fields. Other field names include an abbreviation of the object type included in the field name, such as in Tbl_Invoice. Early database programs required single-word field names. As a result, database developers became creative in naming fields in such a way that the separate words stood out. To overcome cryptic field names, Access uses captions to make the field name more appropriate.

Formatting Data Using Input Masks

You can control and correct data formats using the field property *input mask*—the property that controls the format of field data. Using input masks, you can set the characters that you want to display in fields, such as the parentheses in a phone number, and Access formats the field regardless of how people type the data. Consistency of data format is important not only for visual aesthetics, but also helps ensure accurate results in searches, queries, and sorts.

Using the Input Mask Wizard

The Input Mask Wizard is a valuable tool for setting input mask format. Access has identified many of the most common formats required in databases and has included them among the options presented by the Wizard so that you can select the format you want to use. You select a field format that displays the characters you want to include in data and Access adds the characters to data that data entry personnel enter. You can also set input masks to require a specific number of characters in a field and to convert characters to CAPITAL or lowercase. By setting an input mask for a field, you ensure that data format in tables is consistent. Because table data is consistent, data displayed in forms, reports, and other objects is also consistent.

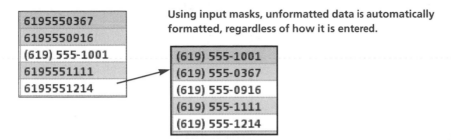

Using input masks, unformatted data is automatically formatted, regardless of how it is entered.

A build ⊡ button appears at the right end of the Input Mask box when you click the box. This button starts the Input Mask Wizard that helps you build the mask.

Identifying Input Mask Symbols

When you use the Input Mask Wizard to create input masks for common field formats, Access places the necessary coding into the Field Properties pane. Access uses several symbols to control the appearance of data as described in the following table.

QUICK REFERENCE	FORMATTING DATA USING INPUT MASK SYMBOLS	
Symbol	**Description**	**Example**
0	Requires a numeric digit.	(000) 000-0000 requires the area code as part of the phone number.
9	Restricts, but does not require, data to a digit.	(999) 000-0000 requires the seven-digit phone number without the three digit area code. If the area code is included, it must be numeric. Plus and minus signs are not allowed.
#	Restricts data to a digit, +, -, or space.	#99.99 permits + or – in the position of the #.
L	Requires an alphabetic character.	LL requires the entry of two alphabetic characters in the State field.
?	Restricts, but does not require, data to alphabetic characters.	L????L requires two characters, one on each end of the data, but permits four additional alphabetic characters between.
A	Requires an alphabetic or numeric character.	AAA-AAAA permits a phone number to be entered either as 555-1234 or 555-HOME or Holiday.
a	Allows, but does not require, alphabetic or numeric characters.	(aaa) AAA-AAAA requires the seven-character phone number but not the area code.
&	Requires any character, alphabetic or numeric, or a space.	&&&& permits data entry such as a four-character ID that could be TCO1 or X 43 or 1234.
C	Allows, but does not require, any character or space.	CCCC could contain TCO1, TCO, TC23, TC 2, and so forth.
.,:;-/	Six characters used to separate parts of numeric, date, time, and currency values.	#,###.## permits numeric data separating dollars from cents and thousands from hundreds.
<	Converts characters to lowercase.	<aaaaa permits entry of five characters such as *ABCDE* and converts data to lowercase *abcde*. One additional control symbol must follow the < for each allowable character you want formatted in lowercase.

Symbol	Description	Example
>	Converts characters to uppercase.	>aaaaa permits entry of five characters such as *abcde* and converts the data to *ABCDE*. One additional control symbol must follow the > for each allowable character you want formatted in uppercase.
!	Displays the input mask characters from right to left.	!(#) 000-0000 would right-align the phone number so that if only seven numbers are entered, the area code is left blank. This affects fields defined with the Number data type.
\	Causes characters that follow the \ to display as a literal character rather than an instruction.	(\A) would appear as (A).
"Literal Text"	Places text that appears between the quotation marks into the field value at the identified position.	"TC-"0000 places the TC- before the numbers entered. In some cases, a space is also enclosed in quotation marks to be sure the space appears in the value.
Password	Creates a password entry text box. Any character typed in the text box is stored as the character but displays as an asterisk (*) as the password is entered.	When 15dice is typed, Access shows ******.

Storing Input Mask Characters

As you navigate through the pages of the Input Mask Wizard, Access will prompt you to make a decision about how you want Access to store table data. Access provides two alternatives for storing the input mask with the table data—with or without the symbols. Storing the symbols with the data increases the size of the electronic database file. Therefore, companies that store extremely large volumes of data often prefer storing the data without the input mask symbols.

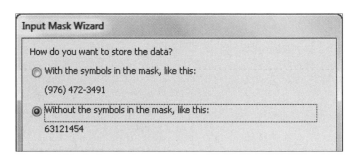

Two options for storing data formatted using input masks.

Using SmartTags

As you work in Access, you will periodically see icons such as the Paste Options SmartTag you may have seen in Word and other Microsoft applications. In Access, SmartTags provide options that enable you to apply changes you make to a field in one object to the same field when it appears in other objects. For example, if you add a field from one table to a form or report and then modify the field properties in the table, the Property Options SmartTag appears so that you can choose to apply the same property changes to the field when it appears in forms and reports. By setting these options, you can ensure the consistency of data across all database objects.

The Property Options SmartTag appears beside the property that changes.

General	Lookup	
Field Size		255
Format		
Input Mask	🟰 ▾	"RCE-"0000
Caption		
Default Value		Update Input Mask everywhere DrID is used
Validation Rule		Help on propagating field properties
Validation Text		
Required		No

Options on the Property Options list enable you to apply the change to update the field in other objects or to obtain help.

DEVELOP YOUR SKILLS 3.4.1

Set Primary Key, Field Size, Captions, and Input Mask Properties

In this exercise, you will work with the Doctors table, which currently has no primary key identified. You will set the primary key, field size, input masks, and captions for fields in the table.

Before You Begin: The Raritan Clinic East—Formatted database should be open.

1. Display the **Doctors** table in Design View.

2. Follow these steps to set a primary key for the Doctors table:

Ⓐ Ensure that the **DrID** field is selected.　　　Ⓑ **Ensure** that the Table Tools Design tab is active.

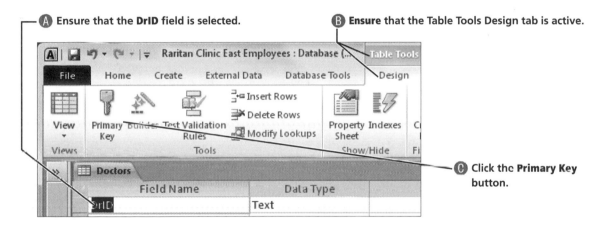

Ⓒ Click the **Primary Key** button.

3. Follow these steps to set the field size for the DrID field:

Ⓐ Click the **field row button** to ensure that the **DrID** field is selected.

Ⓑ **Double-click** the value in the Field Size property and type 7.

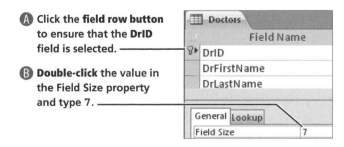

4. Follow these steps to set an input mask for the DrID field:

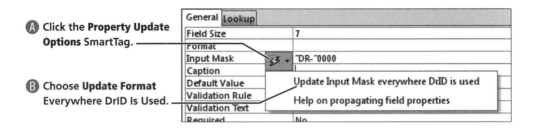

Ⓐ **Ensure** that the DrID field is still selected.

Ⓑ Choose the **Input Mask box** in the Field Properties pane and **type** **"DR-"0000.**

Ⓒ **Press** Tab.

This input mask formats the employee number using DR- (for doctor) followed by a four-digit number. As a result, the data entry person only needs to type the four-digit number and you can set the option to update all instances of the property change. When you move off the Input Mask property, Access adds characters to identify the DR as required text and displays the Property Update Options SmartTag.

5. Follow these steps to select Property Update options:

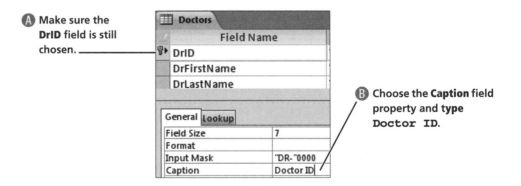

Ⓐ Click the **Property Update Options** SmartTag.

Ⓑ Choose **Update Format Everywhere DrID Is Used.**

Access displays the Update Properties dialog box, which contains a list of all objects using the field. For this field, only one object is listed.

6. Click **Yes** to update the field properties for the field.

7. Follow these steps to change the caption for the field:

Ⓐ Make sure the **DrID** field is still chosen.

Doctors

Field Name
DrID
DrFirstName
DrLastName

General Lookup

Field Size	7
Format	
Input Mask	"DR-"0000
Caption	Doctor ID

Ⓑ Choose the **Caption** field property and **type** **Doctor ID.**

8. **Save** 💾 changes to the table. Choose **Yes** in the warning message to continue.

9. Choose **Design→Views→View** ▦ from the Ribbon to view the datasheet.

Use the Input Mask Wizard

Now you will apply a standard Input Mask format to a field.

10. Switch back to **Design View** and follow these steps to format the DrTelephone number using the Input Mask Wizard:

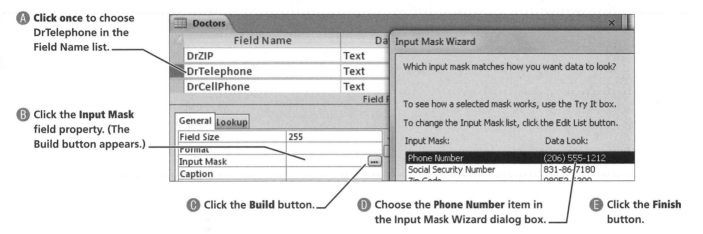

Ⓐ **Click once to choose DrTelephone in the Field Name list.**

Ⓑ **Click the Input Mask field property. (The Build button appears.)**

Ⓒ Click the **Build** button.

Ⓓ Choose the **Phone Number** item in the Input Mask Wizard dialog box.

Ⓔ Click the **Finish** button.

Create Additional Settings

11. Repeat the procedures outlined in **steps 2–9** to assign field size, input mask, and caption properties for additional Doctor table fields, **saving** changes each time you are prompted. Use the Property Update Options SmartTag to apply the changes to the field each time it appears and click **Yes** when advised that data may be lost.

Field	Field Size	Input Mask	Caption
DrFirstName	25	>L<??????????????????????	First Name
DrLastName	25	>L<??????????????????????	Last Name
DrStreet	30		Street Address
DrCity	15	>L<?????????????	City
DrState	2	>LL	State
DrZIP			ZIP
DrWorkExtension	14		Office Phone Extension
DrTelephone	14	Use the Input Mask Wizard and choose the Telephone Format	Home Phone
DrCellPhone	14	Use the Input Mask Wizard and choose the Telephone Format	Cell Phone
DrDateHired			Date Hired
DrDateTerm			Date Terminated
DrDOB			Date of Birth

12. **Save** 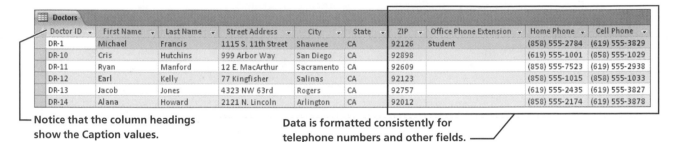 changes to the table, choose **Yes** when advised that some data may be lost, and switch to **Datasheet View** to review the data.
The table should look similar to the following illustration.

Doctor ID	First Name	Last Name	Street Address	City	State	ZIP	Office Phone Extension	Home Phone	Cell Phone
DR-1	Michael	Francis	1115 S. 11th Street	Shawnee	CA	92126	Student	(858) 555-2784	(619) 555-3829
DR-10	Cris	Hutchins	999 Arbor Way	San Diego	CA	92898		(619) 555-1001	(858) 555-1029
DR-11	Ryan	Manford	12 E. MacArthur	Sacramento	CA	92609		(858) 555-7523	(619) 555-2938
DR-12	Earl	Kelly	77 Kingfisher	Salinas	CA	92123		(858) 555-1015	(858) 555-1033
DR-13	Jacob	Jones	4323 NW 63rd	Rogers	CA	92757		(619) 555-2435	(619) 555-3827
DR-14	Alana	Howard	2121 N. Lincoln	Arlington	CA	92012		(858) 555-2174	(619) 555-3878

Notice that the column headings show the Caption values.

Data is formatted consistently for telephone numbers and other fields.

13. **Close** ☒ the table.

Setting Validation Rules

Video Lesson labyrinthelab.com/videos

A validation rule is a field property that enables you to limit the values entered into the field. Setting validation rules helps reduce the errors associated with entering inaccurate or invalid data in a field. You could, for example, limit the value typed into an Hours Worked field to 40 or fewer or the value in the Pay Rate to less than $50 by setting a validation rule. The field *validation rule* property helps you control the specific values entered in a field to prevent invalid data entry.

Setting Appropriate Data Types for Validation Rules

For validation rules to be effective, it is important that the field for which you are setting the rule be formatted appropriately for the data type that should be entered. For example, if you plan to set a validation rule requiring a four-digit number, the data type for the field should be set to Number. If you are requiring dates that occur before a specific date, the data type for the field should be Date/Time.

Setting Validation Text for Rules

When you set a validation rule for a field, it is also a good idea to set *validation text*. Validation text contains instructions or valid data values to help guide the person entering data. Access displays the text as a message each time data entry personnel enter an invalid value in the field.

Setting Different Types of Validation Rules

Validation rules are used to compare data entered into table fields whether you use the table or form to enter values. For numeric values, you can set comparison rules so that Access determines how the value entered compares to values you consider valid. Samples of comparisons Access can determine are shown in the following table:

Comparison	Validation Rule Example	Validation Text Example
Greater than	>100	Please enter a value greater than 100.
Less than	<100	Please enter a value less than 100.
Equal to	=100	Please enter a value of 100.
Date before a date	<#1/1/2008#	Please enter a date before the year 2008.
Greater than or equal to	>=100	Please enter a value of 100 or more.
Less than or equal to	<=100	Please enter a value of 100 or less.
Like	Like "TC-0000"	Please enter a 4-digit value starting with TC-.
Between	Between 0 and 10	Departments range from 1 to 9. Please enter a value from 1 to 9.

The same wildcards used to enter input masks are used in validation rules. For example, the question mark is substituted for each character that is required but may vary, such as in DR-???. The asterisk (*) can substitute for a group of characters that may vary, such as in DR-*.

Set Validation Rules

In this exercise, you will set validation rules for data entered into fields in the Nurses Aides table.
Before You Begin: The Raritan Clinic East—Formatted database should be open.

1. Display the **Nurses Aides** table in Design View.

2. Follow these steps to set a validation rule for the Department field:

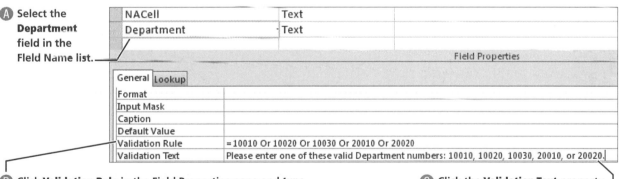

Ⓐ Select the **Department** field in the Field Name list.

Ⓑ Click **Validation Rule** in the Field Properties pane and **type** =10010 Or 10020 Or 10030 Or 20010 Or 20020.

Ⓒ Click the **Validation Text** property and **type** the text shown here.

3. **Save** 💾 changes to the table. Choose **Yes** if advised that data integrity rules have changed and that the process may take a long time.

4. Choose **Design→Views→View** 🧾 from the Ribbon.

Test the New Validation Rules

5. Follow these steps to test the validation rule just set:

(A) **Select** any value in the Department field and type **30010**.

(B) **Press** Tab to move to the next field and to display the validation text entered.

(C) Click **OK** to acknowledge the message and then type **20010** and press Tab.

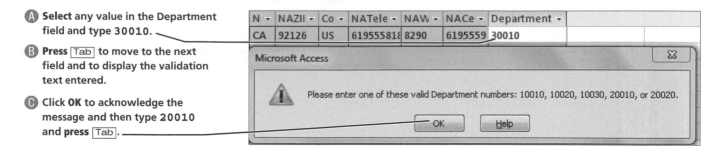

6. **Save** changes to the table.

Setting Default Field Values

Video Lesson   labyrinthelab.com/videos

Validation rules control the data you enter in table fields. Setting *default values* for field data automatically enters data into a field and can help reduce the number of errors made during data entry. While default values are impractical for some fields, they work well when most records contain the same data in a field.

Example

Most of the employees at the Raritan Clinic East live in the same state. As a result, you can enter a default value for the State field. The default value appears in the field whenever a new record is added but is not required for the field (not a validation requirement). If an employee happens to live in a different state, you simply type the new state in the field to replace the default value.

DEVELOP YOUR SKILLS 3.4.3
Set Default Values

In this exercise, you will set a default value for the State field in the Nurses Aides table.

Before You Begin: The Raritan Clinic East—Formatted database should be open.

1. Display the **Nurses Aides** table in Design View.

2. Follow these steps to create a default value for the NAState field:

(A) Select the **NAState** field in the Field Name column.

(B) Select **Default Value** in the Field Properties pane and type **CA**.

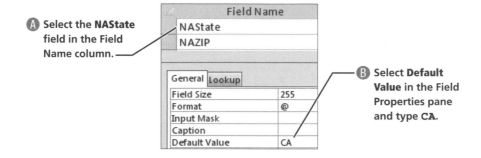

Access adds the quotation marks when you press Tab *or save the table.*

3. **Save**  changes to the table.

4. Choose **Design→Views→View** ⊞ on the Ribbon to display the datasheet.

5. Click the **Last Record** ⊪ navigation button to move to the bottom of the datasheet and review the datasheet shown here:

Access places the default value in the last row of the table datasheet so that you know it is active. You can replace this value, if necessary, the next time you enter a new record, by typing a different state.

Fir Bouleva	San Dieg	CA	55532
		CA	

6. **Close** ☒ the table.

3.5 Retrieving Data

Video Lesson   labyrinthelab.com/videos

The primary purpose of any database is to be able to locate and retrieve data quickly and efficiently. Whether you're processing an order, announcing statistics, or updating records, being able to find the data is important. Access provides three main tools and features for helping to locate and retrieve data:

- Sorting features
- Filtering tools
- Find and Replace

Sorting Records

Access automatically sorts records according to the primary key field identified when a table is created and fields are set up. Many times tables are sorted by record number so that as you enter records, Access assigns a number to the record and the records sort in the order in which you enter them. The database sort feature enables you to rearrange table records on the basis of data found in other table columns. Two main sort orders are available:

- **Sort Ascending**—Arranges data in alphabetical order from A to Z, in numeric order from lowest to highest, or in chronological order from first to last.
- **Sort Descending**—Arranges data in reverse alphabetical order from Z to A, in numeric order from highest to lowest, or in reverse chronological order from last to first.

Sorting Records Using Tables and Forms

Regardless of whether you are working with a table or a form, the primary procedures for sorting records are the same.

Sort Records in a Table

In this exercise, you will sort records in both tables and forms and clear all sorts.

1. Open the **Nurses Aides** table and follow these steps to sort records by last name:

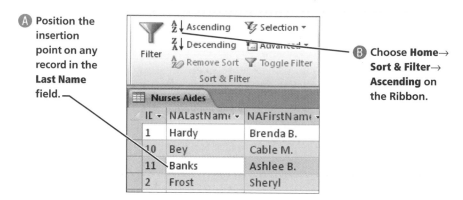

Ⓐ Position the insertion point on any record in the **Last Name** field.

Ⓑ Choose **Home→ Sort & Filter→ Ascending** on the Ribbon.

2. Follow these steps to set a descending sort order and clear all sorts:

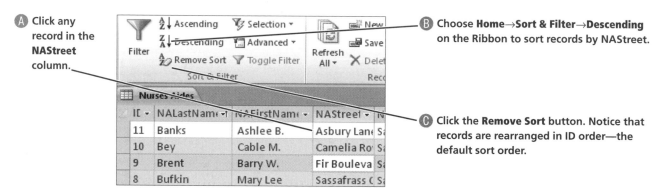

Ⓐ Click any record in the **NAStreet** column.

Ⓑ Choose **Home→Sort & Filter→Descending** on the Ribbon to sort records by NAStreet.

Ⓒ Click the **Remove Sort** button. Notice that records are rearranged in ID order—the default sort order.

3. **Close** ☒ the table.
   Access displays a prompt asking if you wish to save changes to the table. Because you have changed the sort order a couple of times and then cleared the sorts, Access recognizes that you have changed the layout of the table while it was open. As a result, it prompts you to save changes. If you were to click Yes, the changes would become part of the table design. Instead, choose No and discard the changes.

4. Choose **No** in response to the prompt to save the changes.

5. Open the **Raritan Clinic East Doctors** form and follow these steps to sort the doctors:

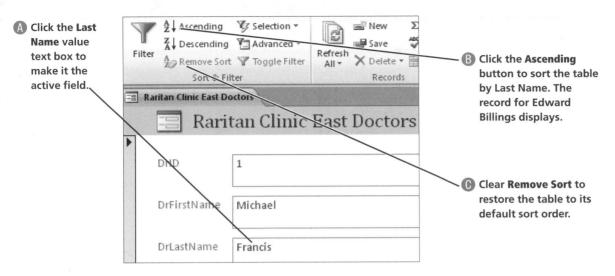

Ⓐ Click the **Last Name** value text box to make it the active field.

Ⓑ Click the **Ascending** button to sort the table by Last Name. The record for Edward Billings displays.

Ⓒ Clear **Remove Sort** to restore the table to its default sort order.

6. **Close** ☒ the form.

Sorting Records Using Multiple Fields

Video Lesson   labyrinthelab.com/videos

Data in Access can be sorted on more than one table field at the same time. This can be useful when sorting fields where the value in the first field of more than one record is the same so you want to select a second field on which to organize the records.

Example

Take, for example, personal names. Many records in a table might contain the same last name value. When this happens, selecting the first name field as a second sort field is often appropriate. Using this example, the last name field would be considered the *primary sort* field, and the first name field is called the *secondary sort* field. The secondary sort field is only considered when multiple records contain the same data in the primary sort field.

Doctor ID ▾	Last Name ▾↑	First Name ▾
DR-8	Billings	Edward
DR-15	Bonifay	Madeline
DR-1	Francis	Michael
DR-6	Good	Ruthann
DR-9	Holland	Elizabeth
DR-14	Howard	Alana
DR-10	Hutchins	Cris

These records are sorted first by Last Name column and then by First Name.

How Multiple Column Sorts Work

Access sorts data on multiple fields from left to right. As a result, the columns in a table must appear side by side in the datasheet and the column on the left must be the one you want sorted first (primary sort field). Access will then consider the second column (secondary sort field) only when it finds identical values in the primary sort field. You can perform more complex sorts on multiple fields using the Advanced Filter/Sort options, or sort multiple columns by rearranging them in the datasheet so that they appear side by side.

Doctor ID ▾	Last Name ▾↑	First Name ▾
DR-8	Billings	Edward
DR-15	Bonifay	Madeline
DR-1	Francis	Michael
DR-6	Good	Ruthann
DR-9	Holland	Elizabeth
DR-14	Howard	Alana
DR-10	Hutchins	Cris

In order to sort the Last Name field first, it had to be moved to the left of the First Name field.

QUICK REFERENCE   SORTING RECORDS

Task	Procedure
Sort ascending	■ Position the cursor in the field on which you want to sort records. ■ Choose Home→Sort & Filter→Ascending $\boxed{\begin{smallmatrix}A\\Z\end{smallmatrix}\downarrow}$ on the Ribbon.
Sort descending	■ Position the cursor in the field on which you want to sort records. ■ Choose Home→Sort & Filter→Descending $\boxed{\begin{smallmatrix}Z\\A\end{smallmatrix}\downarrow}$ on the Ribbon.
Clear sorts	■ Choose Home→Sort & Filter→Clear All Sorts $\boxed{\begin{smallmatrix}A\\Z\end{smallmatrix}}$ on the Ribbon.
Sort on multiple fields	■ Arrange the fields you want to sort next to each other with the primary field to the left of the secondary field. ■ Select both field column headings and click the sort button for the sort order in which you want to sort the records.

DEVELOP YOUR SKILLS 3.5.2
Sort Records Using Multiple Fields

In this exercise, you will sort data in a table on the basis of the values found in two columns.

1. Open the **Doctors** table in the Raritan Clinic East—Formatted database.

2. Follow these steps to sort table records on the basis of values contained in multiple fields:

Ⓐ Click the **First Name** column heading and drag the mouse to select the Last Name column heading so that both columns are selected.

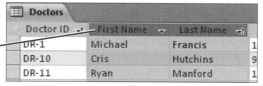

Ⓑ Choose **Home→Sort & Filter→Ascending** on the Ribbon.

3. Review the record sort results.

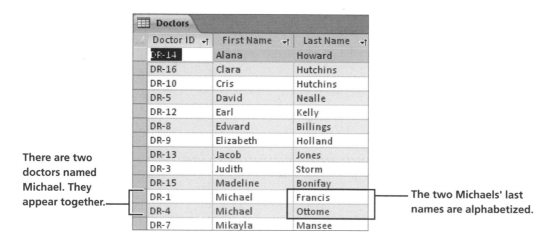

There are two doctors named Michael. They appear together.

The two Michaels' last names are alphabetized.

4. **Clear** all sort orders and click any value in the Street column to deselect both columns.

5. Follow these steps to sort on the same two columns and obtain different results:

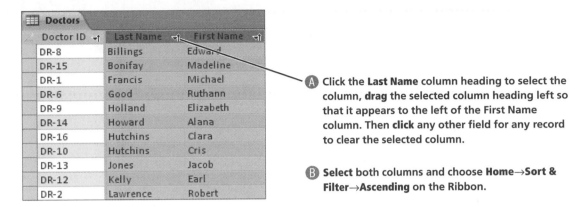

A Click the **Last Name** column heading to select the column, **drag** the selected column heading left so that it appears to the left of the First Name column. Then **click** any other field for any record to clear the selected column.

B **Select** both columns and choose **Home→Sort & Filter→Ascending** on the Ribbon.

Notice that the records now appear in alphabetical order by last name—the Hutchins names are together and alphabetical by first name.

6. **Close** ☒ the table. Choose **No** when prompted to save the changes.

Locating and Deleting Records Using Table Datasheets

Video Lesson labyrinthelab.com/videos

The navigation buttons found at the bottom of tables and forms provide an efficient way to move among records when the number of records in a database is relatively few. When a database contains large volumes of data, finding a more efficient way to locate records becomes important. Both tables and forms are the primary objects used to locate records for updating and deleting.

QUICK REFERENCE	DELETING RECORDS
Task	**Procedure**
Delete a record	Use one of the following procedures to delete a record: ■ Click the record selector button at the left end of the record and press ⌷Delete⌷ on the keyboard to remove the record. Then choose Yes when warned that you are about to delete a record. ■ Choose Home→Records→More ▦ on the Ribbon and choose Delete.

Using Find and Replace

The Find and Replace tool in Access improves the efficiency of maintaining a database that constantly changes. Using the tool, you can locate records easily and then delete them or edit them.

The Find page of the Find and Replace dialog box contains a few features similar to those found in other Microsoft applications. Because data stored in a database is somewhat different from the text and data stored in other files, you will find some unique fields as you work in Access.

FROM THE KEYBOARD
⌷Ctrl⌷+⌷F⌷ to open the Find page of the Find and Replace dialog box

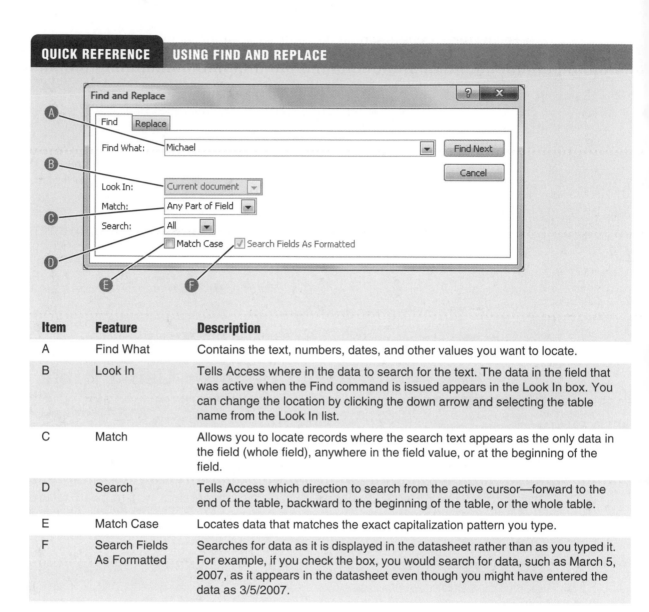

Item	Feature	Description
A	Find What	Contains the text, numbers, dates, and other values you want to locate.
B	Look In	Tells Access where in the data to search for the text. The data in the field that was active when the Find command is issued appears in the Look In box. You can change the location by clicking the down arrow and selecting the table name from the Look In list.
C	Match	Allows you to locate records where the search text appears as the only data in the field (whole field), anywhere in the field value, or at the beginning of the field.
D	Search	Tells Access which direction to search from the active cursor—forward to the end of the table, backward to the beginning of the table, or the whole table.
E	Match Case	Locates data that matches the exact capitalization pattern you type.
F	Search Fields As Formatted	Searches for data as it is displayed in the datasheet rather than as you typed it. For example, if you check the box, you would search for data, such as March 5, 2007, as it appears in the datasheet even though you might have entered the data as 3/5/2007.

Locate and Delete Records in a Table

In this exercise, you will use Find to locate a record in a table and delete it.

1. Open the **Doctors** table in the Raritan Clinic East—Formatted database.

2. Follow these steps to find the record to delete:

A Choose **Home→Find→Find** on the Ribbon to display the Find and Replace dialog box.

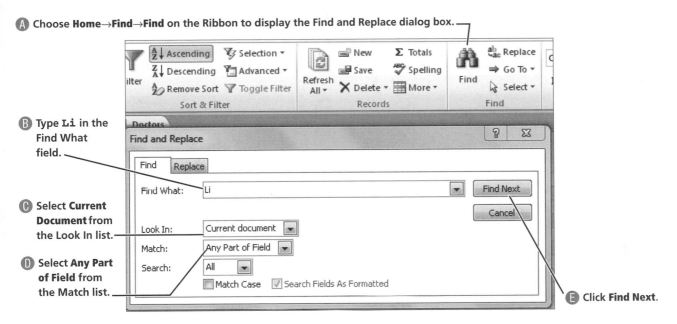

B Type **Li** in the Find What field.

C Select **Current Document** from the Look In list.

D Select **Any Part of Field** from the Match list.

E Click **Find Next**.

Access finds the record for Earl Kelly who lives in Salinas. If you saved the table after sorting it in a previous exercise, you may have to click the Find Next button two or three times to locate Earl Kelly's record.

3. Click **Cancel** to close the Find and Replace dialog box, and then follow these steps to delete the Earl Kelly record:

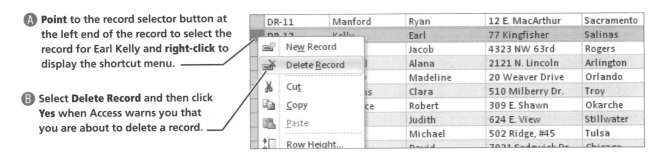

A **Point** to the record selector button at the left end of the record to select the record for Earl Kelly and **right-click** to display the shortcut menu.

B Select **Delete Record** and then click **Yes** when Access warns you that you are about to delete a record.

Leave the table open.

Using Forms to Locate and Edit Records

Video Lesson labyrinthelab.com/videos

Tables are one type of object you can use to update or delete records from a database. You can also use forms to edit and delete records. The basic procedures required to locate records using a form are the same as those used to locate records in a table.

DEVELOP YOUR SKILLS 3.5.4
Locate and Edit Records in a Form

In this exercise, you will locate a record using a form and update the data contained in the record.

1. Open the **Doctors** form in the Raritan Clinic East—Formatted database.

2. Choose **Home→Find→Find** 🔍 on the Ribbon and follow these steps to locate the record to edit:

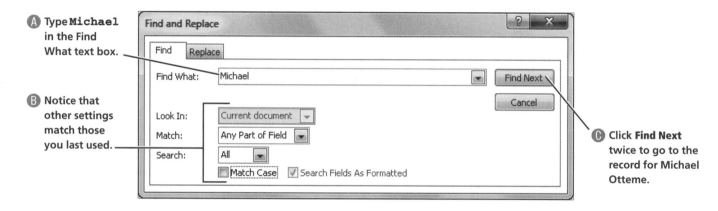

Ⓐ Type **Michael** in the Find What text box.

Ⓑ Notice that other settings match those you last used.

Ⓒ Click **Find Next** twice to go to the record for Michael Otteme.

3. Click **Cancel** to close the Find and Replace dialog box and then **type** the following new value in the First Name field to replace the current contact name: **John.**

4. **Close** ☒ the form.

Using Find and Replace to Update Records

Video Lesson labyrinthelab.com/videos

FROM THE KEYBOARD

Ctrl+H for Find and Replace

When you have specific edits to make to individual records, locating the records and making the edits works well. There are times when you need to update the data in one table field for multiple records with the identical replacement data. For example, when the area code for a city changes, multiple records would need to be updated with the same value. The Replace command enables you to update records in cases such as this by replacing existing data with new data. Because you are already familiar with the options on the Find page of the Find and Replace dialog box, you'll find the Replace page of the dialog box very familiar. The Replace action buttons are used to:

- **Replace**—Replace text for each occurrence of the search text one at a time.
- **Replace All**—Replace all occurrences of the search text with the new text at the same time.

In general, the Replace All command should be used with great caution to avoid unexpected results. For example, if you search for a string of characters such as *the* and replace those letters with the single character *a* using Replace All, you may find that Access will replace the characters in *their* so that it becomes *air*. Both are valid words.

DEVELOP YOUR SKILLS 3.5.5
Update Multiple Records Using Find and Replace

In this exercise, you will use the Find and Replace dialog box to update multiple records with the same data.

1. Open the **Doctors** table in the Raritan Clinic East—Formatted database.

2. Follow these steps to locate and replace text with new values:

Ⓐ Choose **Home→Find→Replace** on the Ribbon. ⎯⎯⎯⎯⎯⎯⎯

Ⓑ Type **619** in the Find What text box and **858** in the Replace With text box.

Ⓒ Change other settings to appear as shown here.

Ⓓ Click **Replace All.**

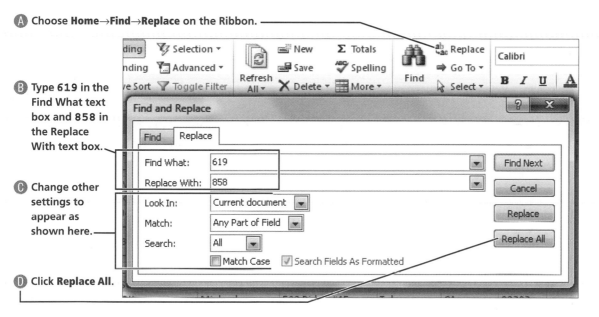

Access presents a warning message advising you that you will not be able to undo this action.

3. Choose **Yes** in response to the warning prompt, click **Cancel** to close the dialog box, and then scroll to the right to ensure that the value in the Home Phone field for all records shows 858.

4. **Close** ☒ the table.

Filtering Records

Video Lesson   labyrinthelab.com/videos

So far, you have sorted records to place them in an order that they are more easily reviewed, and have used the Find and Replace features to delete and update records. In both cases, you worked with all records contained in the table. When you work with large volumes of table data, there will be times when you want to locate a group of records that contain specific values in specific fields. Filtering enables you to select a subset of records contained in the table to make working with the records more efficient.

Using the Filter Tools

The Filter tool enables you to identify a value in any table field and tell Access to select only those records in the datasheet that contain the same value in the selected field. This process applies a *filter* to the table that hides records when the data in the active field contains different data. For example, if you work with a database that contains thousands of records for consumers across the country, you could apply a filter to identify all the people who live in a specific state.

Access provides two types of methods for filtering records: Filter by Selection and Filter by Form.

- **Filter by Selection**—Selects records on the basis of the value contained in the active field for the active record.
- **Filter by Form**—Selects records on the basis of values or conditions (criteria) that you type in one or more form fields. Again, Access searches only the fields you specify to find the match.

You will explore both techniques in this section.

Filtering Records by Selection

When you filter database records by selection, you have two options. You can instruct Access to select all records containing data that matches the value or selected text in the active field of the selected record. You can also instruct Access to select all records containing any value other than the one selected. Access searches only the active field to find the matches.

Removing a Filter

When you filter records in a table, Access recognizes the change to the display. As a result, if you close the table without removing the filter, Access prompts you to save changes to the table. Many times, you do want to save changes—such as when you widen or hide columns. Normally, filtering data in a table is temporary while you work with the data, so you do not want to save a filtered table. You remove a filter using the Toggle Filter tool.

Using the Toggle Filter Tool

The Toggle Filter ▼ tool in the Sort & Filter section of the Ribbon serves two purposes:

- After you apply a filter, clicking the Toggle Filter ▼ button removes the filter and displays all records.
- After removing a filter, clicking the Toggle Filter ▼ button reapplies the last filter applied.

In addition, when you point to the Toggle Filter button, a ToolTip displays to let you know what action you are performing. For example, when you point to the Toggle Filter button after applying a filter, the ToolTip shows *Remove Filter*. When you point to the Toggle Filter button after removing a filter, the ToolTip shows *Apply Filter*.

Filter Records by Selection

Two records in the Nurses Aides table contain invalid ZIP codes. In this exercise, you will filter the records in the table, correct the ZIP code, and then remove the filter.

1. Open the **Nurses Aides** table in the Raritan Clinic East —Formatted database.

2. Follow these steps to set a filter:

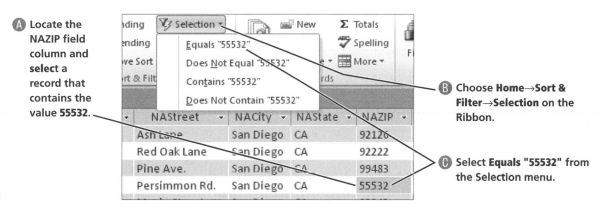

Ⓐ **Locate the NAZIP field column and select a record that contains the value 55532.**

Ⓑ **Choose Home→Sort & Filter→Selection on the Ribbon.**

Ⓒ **Select Equals "55532" from the Selection menu.**

Access applies the filter immediately and displays two records that contain the value.

3. Click the **NAZIP** field for each of the two records and type **95532** as the ZIP code for both records.

4. Click the **Toggle Filter** button to remove the filter and display all table records.

5. **Close** the table. Choose **No** when prompted to save changes.

Filtering Records by Form

Video Lesson   labyrinthelab.com/videos

Filtering records by form enables you to set criteria in fields of a blank form. Access then filters the database to select only the records that contain values set in fields on the form. One advantage to using the Filter By Form feature is that you can select records on the basis of values in multiple fields without rearranging the layout of table fields. Another advantage is that you can use comparison indicators to locate records that fit within a range of values. When you filter by form, Access remembers the sort criteria. As a result, it is important to clear all filters after you apply this filter.

Identifying Comparison Operators

When you use the Filter By Form feature in Access, you will often apply comparison operators so that Access can locate records that contain the data you want to find. These operators are identified and described in the following table.

Comparison Symbol	Description
=	Records in the table must contain a value that matches exactly the value you enter in the form for the field set.
<	Records in the table must contain a value less than the value you enter in the form for the field set.
>	Records in the table must contain a value greater than the value you enter in the form for the field set.
<>	Records in the table must contain a value different from the value you enter in the form for the field set.
<=	Records in the table must contain a value less than or equal to the value you set for the field.
>=	Records in the table must contain a value greater than or equal to the value you set for the field.

The format of the Filter By Form entry palette depends on whether you are filtering from a table or from a form. If you are filtering from a table, a datasheet palette opens.

Notice that the table name appears in the Filter by Form tab. ——

When you filter from a table datasheet, a blank datasheet for the table opens.

Down arrows on active fields enable you to select values on the basis of valid table values.

If you are filtering from a form, a blank form opens.

Notice that the form name appears in the Filter by Form tab. ——

Down arrows on fields enable you to select values from a list of valid table values. ——

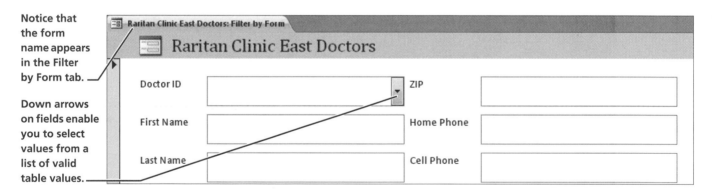

Using Wildcards

Because database users often want to locate records that contain data in a specific field but may also contain additional text or data, Access accepts the use of *wildcards*, such as the asterisk, for setting criteria. Valid wildcards and how Access uses them are identified in the following table.

Wildcard	Example	Description
*		Appears in a position where any number of additional characters may appear in a search string.
	Graham	Locates all records with the string of text *graham* somewhere in the field value. The asterisk allows text and other data characters to appear before the search string as well as after the search text, regardless of how many characters appear.
	Graham*	Locates all records with the string of text *graham* at the beginning of the field value regardless of how many characters follow it.
	*Graham	Locates all records with the string of text *graham* at the end of the field value regardless of how many characters precede it.
	Gra*ham	Locates all records with the string of text beginning *gra* and ending *ham* regardless of how many characters appear between the search strings.
?		Each question mark represents a character and limits the search to a specified number of characters on the basis of the number of question marks that appear.
	Gra?am	Locates all records with the string of text *gra* at the beginning of the field value and *am* at the end of the field value with only one letter between the instances of the letter *a* in the search string.
	Gra???	Locates all records with the string of text *gra* at the beginning of the field value followed by three additional characters.

Filter Records by Form

In this exercise, you will use tables to filter records by form.

1. Open the **Nurses Aides** table in the Raritan Clinic East—Formatted database.

2. Follow these steps to open Filter by Form:

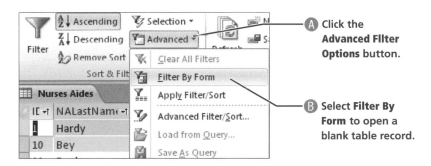

Ⓐ Click the **Advanced Filter Options** button.

Ⓑ Select **Filter By Form** to open a blank table record.

3. Follow these steps to filter and select all records in the Nurses Aides table for aides living in ZIP area 99483:

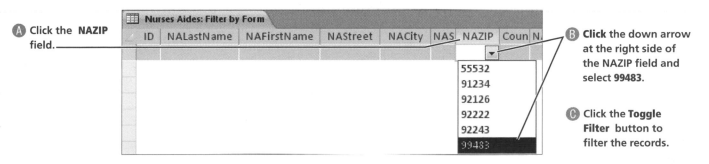

Ⓐ Click the **NAZIP** field.

Ⓑ **Click** the down arrow at the right side of the NAZIP field and select **99483**.

Ⓒ Click the **Toggle Filter** button to filter the records.

Access locates two records that meet the criteria set and places a filter icon beside each field name for the filter values set.

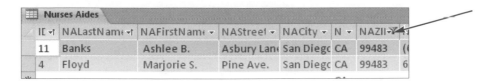

4. Review the results shown above and then choose **Home→Sort & Filter→Toggle Filter** to remove the filter.

5. **Close** ☒ the Nurses Aides table. Choose **No** when prompted to save the changes.

6. **Close** the database and **exit** Access.

3.6 Previewing and Printing Data

Video Lesson   labyrinthelab.com/videos

Reports are considered a primary output format for Access databases because they summarize data and display it as meaningful information. There may be times when you want to print raw data contained in a table or query results datasheet, or data contained in specific fields in a database table. You may also want to print a single record within a database in form layout. Access provides tools for printing all of these objects.

Setting Up Data to Print

Earlier in this lesson you learned how to adjust the column layout on a datasheet, how to search for records containing specific data, and how to filter out records that contain data different from the values you want to display. Each of these activities changes the display of data in a datasheet. When you print from a table datasheet, Access prints the data that actually appears in the datasheet when you issue the print command. You can hide columns to prevent them from printing, change the page layout settings to print the datasheet in landscape layout, and change the margins to fit a datasheet on a single sheet of paper.

3.7 Concepts Review

Concepts Review   labyrinthelab.com/acc10

To check your knowledge of the key concepts introduced in this lesson, complete the Concepts Review quiz by going to the URL listed above. If your classroom is using Labyrinth eLab, you may complete the Concepts Review quiz from within your eLab course.

Reinforce Your Skills

Adjust Datasheet Layout

A new database has been created for Raritan Clinic East. It contains a table that lists patients for the clinic as well as some of the drugs that are administered. In this exercise, you will adjust the widths of columns in each table to display data appropriately, reposition fields displayed on the datasheet, and hide other fields to obtain a printout of specific data. After you make the changes required, you can print the datasheets.

1. **Start** Access, and then **open** the rs-Raritan Clinic East Patients database from the Lesson 03 folder in your file storage location.

2. **Enable content**, and choose **File→Save Database As**.

3. **Save** the file using the filename **Raritan Clinic East—End** in the Lesson 03 folder.

Adjust the Datasheet Column Width

4. **Open** the Patients table and **press** Ctrl+A to select all fields and data in the datasheet.

5. **Point** to the border between two of the column headings so the mouse pointer appears as a double-arrow, and then **double-click** the right column headings border between the column headings to widen all the columns to fit the data.

6. Click the **Save** 🖫 button to save changes to the table layout.

Enter Data into the Datasheet

7. Click the **New Record** button to create a new blank record and **enter** the following data to create two additional records:

First Name	Last Name	Street	City	State	ZIP	Telephone	DOB
Alex	KELLY	Olson Avenue	COLUMBUS	OH	43221	6145551024	9/14/2005
Bryan	SANDERS	Quaker Ridge Lane	CHARLESTON	WV	25301		11/22/2000

Now you will hide one of the columns.

8. **Right-click** the Telephone column heading to display the shortcut menu and select **Hide Fields**.

Preview and Print the Table

9. Choose **File→Print→Print** Preview to view the datasheet as it would print and then **print** the document (optional).

10. Click the **Close Print Preview** button to close the preview, **close** the table, **saving** changes if prompted, and close the database.

Close Print Preview

Locate, Filter, and Print Records

A new record needs to be added to the General Employees table in the rs-Raritan Clinic East —End data-base. In this exercise you will locate all records for employees in the department and preview and print a copy of the datasheet.

1. **Open** the rs-Raritan Clinic East Employees database from the Lesson 03 folder and **save** a copy of it as **rs-Raritan Clinic East—EmpEnd**.

2. Open the **General Employees** table.

Find and Filter Records

3. Choose **Home→Find→Find** on the Ribbon and type **Office Adm.** (including the period) in the Find What text box, select **Current Document** from the Look In drop-down list, and then choose **Find Next**.

4. Click **Cancel** to close the Find and Replace dialog box.

5. Choose **Home→Sort & Filter→Selection** on the Ribbon and select the **Equals "Office Adm."** command to filter the records.
   Access locates only two records that contain the value.

Preview and Print Records

6. Choose **File→Print→Print Preview** to preview the datasheet print page.

7. Choose **Print Preview→Print→Print** on the Ribbon to print the datasheet.

8. Choose the **Pages** option in the Print dialog box, **enter** From **1** to **1** and click **OK** to print the two records.

9. **Close** the print preview window and the table.

Sort and Print Datasheets and Reports

One of the benefits of storing data in a database is the ease with which you can sort the data. The US Postal Service requires that bulk mail be sorted and arranged by ZIP code before it will be accepted. Businesses, of course, often send letters to their customers and clients. Valley Hospital wants to use the database to organize records by ZIP code before using it to print envelope labels. In this exercise, you will sort the records by ZIP code and save changes to the table settings so that the records will remain organized in this sort order. In addition, because you have added a new employee to the database, you need to print a copy of the Employee Phone List report.

1. **Open** the rs-Raritan Clinic East—EmpEnd database, and **open** the Patients table (not the Patient Information form).

2. **Hide** the Street column in the datasheet.

Sort Records

3. Place the insertion point in the **ZIP** field for any record.

4. Choose **Home→Sort & Filter→Ascending** ⬛ on the Ribbon to sort the records.
   Access sorts records so that all records with no data in the ZIP field appear at the top of the datasheet.

5. **Press** [Ctrl]+[S] to **save** changes to the table and then **close** it.

6. Open the **Patients** table again to ensure that the sort order was saved, and then **print** a copy of the datasheet.

Preview and Print a Report

7. **Close** the table and **open** the Employee Phone List report; **preview** and **print** the report.

8. **Close** all open database objects and then **close** the database.

Modify Tables and Set Field Properties

The JLD Pharmaceutical Company is building a database that currently contains five tables and two forms. They have entered a few records to test the properties they added to tables as they built them and to determine if the forms work properly. They have discovered edits that must be made to the tables to display data properly. In this exercise, you will set field properties in a table and delete a field from the table.

1. **Open** the rs-JLD Pharmaceuticals Expenses database from the Lesson 03 folder and **save** the database using the filename **rs-JLD Pharmaceuticals Rev**.

2. **Open** the Navigation Pane, **right-click** the Employees table, and choose **Design View** from the shortcut menu.

3. Follow these steps to set an Input Mask property for the EmployeeNumber field:

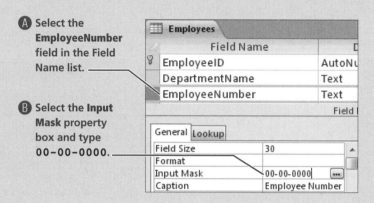

Ⓐ Select the **EmployeeNumber** field in the Field Name list.

Ⓑ Select the **Input Mask** property box and type **00-00-0000**.

4. Click the **Property Update Options SmartTag** and choose **Update Input Mask Everywhere EmployeeNumber** is used. Click **Yes** to accept the default selections.

5. Repeat the procedures outlined in **steps 3–4** to set the following input masks for associated fields in the Employees table, placing enough question marks in the FirstName and LastName input masks to fill up the text box and update using the SmartTag when prompted.

Field	Input Mask
FirstName	>L<?????????????????????????
LastName	>L<????????????????????????
StateOrProvince	>L>L

6. Select the **StateOrProvince** field in the Field Name list and replace the field name by typing **State**.

7. **Save** 🖫 changes to the table. Select the **HomePhone** field in the Field Name list, and then select the **Input Mask** property.

8. Click the **Build** ⟦…⟧ button at the right end of the property, **select** the first format in the Input Mask Wizard dialog box, and click **Finish**.

9. Repeat the procedures outlined in **steps 6–8** to create an input mask for the WorkPhone field, **saving** changes to the table when prompted.

10. Click the **field selector button** for the Country field in the Field Name list and **press** Delete. Choose **Yes** to confirm the field deletion.

11. Select the **State** field and type **WA** in the Default Value property.

12. **Close** the Employees Table and **save** 🖫 changes when prompted.

REINFORCE YOUR SKILLS 3.5
Set a Primary Key

One table in the JLD Pharmaceutical Company database is now displaying data properly. With a few additional modifications, you will have the database ready. In this exercise, you will set a primary key for two tables, Expense Categories and Expense Details.

Before You Begin: Your rs-JLD Pharmaceuticals Rev database should be open.

1. **Right-click** the Expense Categories table and select **Design View**.

2. Select the **ExpenseCategoryID** field.

3. Choose **Design→Tools→Primary Key** on the Ribbon to make the field the key field.

4. **Save** 🖫 changes to the table, and then **close** ⊠ it.

5. **Repeat** the procedures outlined in steps 2–4 to display the Expense Details table in Design View and make the ExpenseDetailID field the key field.

6. **Save** 🖫 changes to the table, and then **close** ⊠ it.

Create a Lookup Field

Table fields in the JLD Pharmaceutical Company database are now completed and you can set some features to simplify data entry. In this exercise, you will create a lookup field in the Expense Reports table that looks up the employee number from the Employees table.

Before You Begin: Your rs-JLD Pharmaceuticals Rev database should be open.

1. **Right-click** the Expense Reports table and select **Design View**.

2. Select the **EmployeeID** field in the Field Name list and **press** Tab to move to the Data Type column.

3. Click the **Data Type** list button and select **Lookup Wizard**.

4. Make the following selections from Lookup Wizard screens, clicking **Next** to advance to the next screen:

   ■ Screen 1: Select the **I Want the Lookup Column to Look Up the Values in a Table or Query**.

   ■ Screen 2: Select the **Table: Employees** option.

   ■ Screen 3: Move **LastName** and **EmployeeID** fields to the Selected Fields list.

   ■ Screen 4: Select **LastName** for the field on which to sort in Ascending order.

   ■ Screen 5: Take no action.

   ■ Screen 6: Accept the default name and choose **Finish**.

5. Choose **Yes** when prompted to save the table.

Test the Lookup Field

6. Choose **Home→Views→View** ▦ on the Ribbon to display the table datasheet.

7. **Press** Tab to move to the Employee ID field and click the **list button** for the first record to view the lookup values list.

8. **Close** the table and the database.

Apply Your Skills

Modify Table Layout, Sort and Filter Records, and Delete Records

Sales from the VonHamburg Tomb, on online shop, have been doing well; therefore, in this exercise, you will need to update the database to remove records. By first filtering the records by form, you can narrow the list of records displayed to make the update process easier. As you work, you will need to adjust datasheet column widths to fit column contents. You will notice that the data is just raw data; for example, dollar signs have not been added.

1. **Launch** Access and **open** the as-VonHamburg Tomb database from the Lesson 03 folder in your file storage location.

2. **Enable content**, and **save** the database to the Lesson 03 folder as a new file named **as-VonHamburg Tomb-end** using the current file format.

Format Table Layout and Sort Data

3. Open the **Records** table, and adjust the column widths of all fields in the table to fit the contents.

4. **Scroll** to the right side of the table until you see both the Selling Price and Date End field columns, and then move the Date End column and place it just to the left of the Selling Price column.

5. **Save** changes to the table, and then **sort** the records alphabetically by the Item Title field.

Filter Records by Form

6. Click the **Advanced Filter Options** button and choose **Filter By Form** to open a blank records form.

7. Type **Decca*** in the Item Title field and **>8/30/07** in the Date End field.

8. Choose **Home→Sort & Filter→Toggle Filter** on the Ribbon.
   Access locates two records.

Select and Delete Records

9. Click the **record selector button** for the first record and then **press** [Shift] and click the **second record selector** button to select both records.

10. **Press** [Delete] to delete both records.
    Access prompts you to confirm the deletion.

11. Choose **Yes** to delete both records.

12. **Clear** the filter criteria using the Advanced Filter Options shortcut menu.

13. **Close** the Records table. Choose **Yes** when prompted to save the table.

Locate and Update Data, and Print Datasheets

New items have been located that need to be added to the VonHamburg Tomb store. They fit into two separate categories, Comics and Collectibles. In addition, the item descriptions of some of the comics and books contain extraneous characters that need to be removed. In this exercise, you will be able to print datasheets that display more uniform data.

1. **Open** the as-VonHamburg Tomb-end database created in the last exercise and then **open** the Comics table.

2. **Adjust** the field column widths of fields containing truncated data and **save** changes to the layout.

Add Records

3. **Add** a new record to the table and **type** the following data into appropriate fields of the new record. Note that not all fields contain data:

Format	A
Title	Marvel—Spider-Man
Category	4542
Store Category	2961949
Quantity	1
Start Price	5
Duration	7
Selling Price	
Gallery Type	Gallery
Shipping Type	Flat
Shipping Service	9
Shipping Service	5
Dispatch Time Max	2

4. **Open** the List Collectibles form, **create** a new blank record in the form, and **enter** the following data for a new item:

Selling Format	S
Accept Offer	Y
Item Title	Masonic Ceremonial Sword
Starting Price	25
Selling Price	
Postage	15
Insurance	10
Date Listed	07/28/2007
Duration	30
Date End	08/27/2007

5. Close the List Collectibles form, saving changes if prompted.

Locate and Update Records

6. Open the **Comics** table, **sort** the table data alphabetically on the Title field, and **locate** the records at the top of the table that contain multiple asterisks.

7. Select the **Title** field of each record containing multiple asterisks and **remove** the asterisks.

 If you accidentally delete text other than the asterisks as you update the records, you can reverse the deletion using the Undo command. Simply press Ctrl+Z to reverse the deletion.

8. Repeat the instructions outlined in **steps 6 and 7** to sort and remove the asterisks from records in the Books table.

9. **Print** copies of the datasheets for the following tables: Collectibles, Records, Books, and Comics.

10. **Close** the database.

APPLY YOUR SKILLS 3.3

Modify Tables and Field Properties

Lagniappe Cruises has a database containing two basic tables—one for cruises and one identifying their ships. The tables are formatted using Text field types and the data needs to be formatted using data types, field properties, etc., so that the data displays properly. In this exercise, you will modify the tables and set field properties.

1. **Open** the as-Lagniappe Cruises database that appears in the Lesson 03 folder and **save** the database using the filename **as-Lagniappe Cruises Rev**.

2. Display the **Cruises** table in Design View and change the field data types to those shown below.

Cruises	
Field Name	Data Type
Ship	Text
Itinerary	Text
InsideCabin	Currency
OutsideCabin	Currency
Verandah	Currency
Destination	Text
SailDate	Text

3. **Save** changes to the table and then display the **table datasheet** to review the data format, responding appropriately to messages that appear.

4. Set the following field properties for the fields identified:

Field	Field Size	Caption
Ship	15	Ship Name
Itinerary	30	
InsideCabin		Inside Cabin
OutsideCabin		Outside Cabin
SailDate		Sail Date

5. Set the following Input Mask, Validation Rule, Validation Text, and Default Value properties for the associated fields:

Field	Input Mask	Validation Rule	Validation Text	Default Value
InsideCabin		>750	The price of these cabins is more than $750. Please enter a value higher than $750.	750
OutsideCabin		>1000	The price of these cabins is more than $1,000. Please enter a value higher than $1,000.	1000
SailDate	00/00/0000;0;_			

6. **Save** 💾 changes to the table, respond appropriately to message boxes, and **print** a copy of the table datasheet.

7. Display the **Ships** table in Design View and set the field data types as shown:

8. Make the ShipID field the **primary key field**.

9. Set the following captions and field sizes for associated fields:

Field Name	Data Type
ShipID	Text
ShipName	Text
Capacity	Number
Length	Number
#InsideCabins	Number
#OutsideCabins	Number
#VerandahCabins	Number
#Decks	Number
DateBuilt	Date/Time

Field	Field Size	Caption
ShipID		Ship ID
ShipName	15	Ship Name
#InsideCabins		Total Inside Cabins
#OutsideCabins		Total Outside Cabins
Verandah		Total Cabins with Verandahs
#Decks		Number Decks
DateBuilt		Date Built

10. **Save** 💾 changes to the table, respond appropriately to message boxes, and **print** a copy of the table datasheet.

Create a Lookup Field

Lagniappe Cruises has a limited number of ships—five. As a result, being able to look up the ship names as you enter data would be helpful. In this exercise, you will create a lookup field that looks up the names of the ships using the Lookup Wizard.

Before You Begin: Your as-Lagniappe Cruises Rev database should be open.

1. Display the **Cruises** table in Design View.

2. Set the data type for the Ship to **Lookup Wizard** and set the following values for the Wizard screens, clicking **Next** to move to the next screen:

   - Screen 1: Select the **I Want the Lookup Column to Look Up Values in a Table or Query** option.
   - Screen 2: Select the **Table: Ships** option.
   - Screen 3: Move the ShipID and ShipName fields to the **Selected Fields** list.
   - Screen 4: Select the **ShipName** field for the sort field and **Ascending** as the sort order.
   - Screen 5: Adjust coloumn widths.
   - Screen 6: Click **Finish**.

3. **Save** ▣ the changes to the table and display the datasheet.

4. Click the **Ship** down arrow for the first record to ensure that the ship names appear.

5. **Close** ✕ all open database objects and **close** the database.

Critical Thinking &
Work-Readiness Skills

In the course of working through the following Microsoft Office-based Critical Thinking exercises, you will also be utilizing various work-readiness skills, some of which are listed next to each exercise. Go to labyrinthelab.com/ workreadiness *to learn more about the work-readiness skills.*

3.1 Sort, Filter, and Locate Records

WORK-READINESS SKILLS APPLIED

- Organizing and maintaining information
- Using computers to process information
- Applying technology to a task

James Elliott found an old database, ct-Service Guild (Lesson 03 folder), once used by Raritan Clinic East. It contains a list of former Service Guild members stored in a table. James can use this database to practice his sorting, filtering, and retrieval skills. Place yourself in James' shoes and review the Members table in the database, adjusting the columns to display all data. Then use the appropriate Access feature to display and print each datasheet that displays all members arranged alphabetically by last name, all members arranged by ZIP code, all members who have paid their dues, all international members, and all members who live in Oregon.

3.2 Get Help on Sorting and Filtering

WORK-READINESS SKILLS APPLIED

- Serving clients/ customers
- Selecting technology
- Organizing and maintaining information

Customer service representatives have asked James to provide them with lists of customers that meet multiple criteria. James turns to the Access Help feature to learn more about advanced searching, sorting, and filtering. Review Access Help or search for help on the web to find out how each of the following Access features might be used:

- Using queries with sorting/filtering
- What to consider when sorting linked tables
- The difference between a simple and complex sort
- The difference between select queries and filters
- How to use advanced filter/sort features

If working in a group, discuss these topics. If working alone, type your responses in a Word document named **ct-Questions** saved to your Lesson 03 folder.

3.3 Sort and Filter Data on the Internet

WORK-READINESS SKILLS APPLIED

- Acquiring and evaluating information
- Interpreting and communicating information
- Thinking creatively

The Human Resources department needs to purchase the most current book on interviewing skills. They have asked that you locate three online bookstores and search each bookstore for their books on interviewing. Print a copy of the first page of each site's search results.

Querying a Database

LESSON OUTLINE

4.1 Creating Select Queries

4.2 Setting Query Criteria

4.3 Sorting a Query and Limiting Results

4.4 Performing Calculations in Queries

4.5 Creating Special Types of Queries

4.6 Concepts Review

Reinforce Your Skills

Apply Your Skills

Critical Thinking & Work-Readiness Skills

LEARNING OBJECTIVES

After studying this lesson, you will be able to:

- Create, save, and run select queries
- Design a query using multiple tables
- Set query criteria
- Define a query sort order
- Create and format a calculated field
- Use functions in query expressions
- Create a crosstab query
- Create unmatched and duplicates queries

One goal of databases is to store data in such a way that it is easy to retrieve records. People in all types of businesses retrieve data and information daily—and often at a moment's notice. When data is stored in tables in a relational database, you can retrieve data and extract records that meet specific criteria using a *query*—a database object used to locate records based on conditions you set.

In this lesson, you will create select, crosstab, and other special queries, set query criteria, and create a form using a query. You will also create and format a calculated field, set a query sort order, set multiple query conditions, and use functions to develop a query expression. Finally, you will create special queries designed to find unmatched records between tables and find duplicate entries in a database table.

Using Queries to Get Answers

After conferring with employees throughout Raritan Clinic East, James Elliott has identified several questions that nurses and other staff are frequently asked:

- How many current patients does a specific doctor have in the clinic?
- Who is a specific patient's doctor?
- Does anyone know a specific nurse's phone number?
- How many current patients are from states other than California?

By identifying questions commonly asked by both callers and staff, James can determine the type of information that is requested of the data contained in the database. As he continues his work at Raritan Clinic East, he begins setting up queries to help human resources answer these and other questions using the database.

Raritan Clinic East

Pediatric Diagnostic Specialists

A query contains fields and criteria used to select records from one or more tables. In this example, the query displays fields from two database tables and searches for all records from the Patients table for Dr. Jones.

Field:	PFirstName	PLastName	PState	Doctor	DrLastName
Table:	Patients	Patients	Patients	Patients	Doctors
Sort:					
Show:	✓	✓	✓	✓	✓
Criteria:					"Jones"
or:					

PFirstName ▾	PLastName ▾↑	PStreet ▾	PCity ▾	PState ▾	PZIP ▾	PTelephone ▾	AdmitDate ▾	Doctor ▾
Kate	Parkington	8235 Honeysuckle St.	Chicago	CA	90698	(858) 555-3465	17-Oct-10	5015
Aubrey	O'Malley	524 Golf Blvd.	San Francisco	CA	96157	(858) 555-8986	10-Oct-10	5004
Christy	Phelps	2520 South Utica St	Denver	CO	80219	(303) 555-3434	11-Oct-10	5007

Patient name fields and state field come from the Patients table.

PFirstName ▾	PLastName ▾	PState ▾	Doctor ▾	Last Name ▾
Aubrey	O'Malley	CA	5004	Jones
Mary	Miquel	CA	5004	Jones
Ada	Ballard	CT	5004	Jones
Ethan	Hawk	CA	5004	Jones
Sarah	Henry	SC	5004	Jones
Christian	Hendon	WI	5004	Jones
Jessica	Rue	CA	5004	Jones
Gabriel	Yu	AK	5004	Jones

Doctor ID ▾	First Name ▾	Last Name ▾
DR-5001	Michael	Francis
DR-5002	Cris	Hutchins
DR-5003	Ryan	Manford
DR-5004	Clara	Hutchins

Doctor ID and last name fields come from the Doctors table. Notice that only patients whose doctor is Dr. Jones are listed in the query results datasheet.

4.1 Creating Select Queries

Video Lesson   labyrinthelab.com/videos

When data is stored in tables in a relational database, you can retrieve data and extract records that meet specific criteria using a *query*—a database object used to locate records on the basis of conditions you set. Not only do queries locate records that meet specific criteria, but they also enable you to select the specific fields of data in database tables that you want to view. As a result, you can display data from selected fields in multiple tables as long as the tables are contained within the same database or linked to the database containing the query.

For example, most businesses have a telephone list of employee phone numbers so that they can reach them in time of need. By creating a select query to display only the employees' names and telephone numbers, the phone list is easy to print in a datasheet layout or report. By saving the query, you can use it again each time you need to print an updated list.

Employee Phone List		
First Name	Last Name	Home Phone
James	Bush	555-4430
Ralph	Johnson	555-2938
Jason	Smith	555-3847
Kay	Chart	555-7162
Becky	Douter	555-0012
Sharon	Fisher	555-1649

A select query showing select fields from the Employees table.

Reviewing Query Features

Some important points about queries to keep in mind:

- A query acts as a saved question you ask a database or as a subset of data from one or more tables.

- Data displayed in the query results datasheet remains stored in its original table rather than in the query.

- When you edit data in a query results datasheet, you are actually editing the data stored in a table.

- Queries are dynamic objects that display up-to-date data stored in database tables.

- Queries can be used to create forms and reports containing fields from multiple tables.

- Query results datasheets enable you to filter or organize data using the same techniques you use to filter and organize table datasheets.

Identifying Tools for Creating Select Queries

The most common type of query is the *select query*. The select query retrieves data from one or more tables and displays the results in a query results datasheet. You can update records that appear in the query results datasheet and use a select query to group records and calculate sums, counts, averages, and other types of totals.

Because of the many different types of queries you may want to create, Access provides two distinct tools for creating queries:

- Query Wizard
- Design view

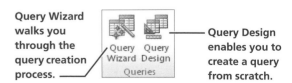

Query Wizard walks you through the query creation process.

Query Design enables you to create a query from scratch.

Buttons for creating queries are grouped on the Queries section of the Ribbon Create tab. You will use both tools to create queries.

Create a Select Query Using the Query Wizard

In this exercise, you will create a select query using the Query Wizard to create a telephone list of Raritan Clinic East nurses.

1. **Open** the Raritan Clinic East database from the Lesson 04 folder and **save** it as a new database named **Raritan Clinic East Queries**.

2. Follow these steps to activate the Query Wizard:

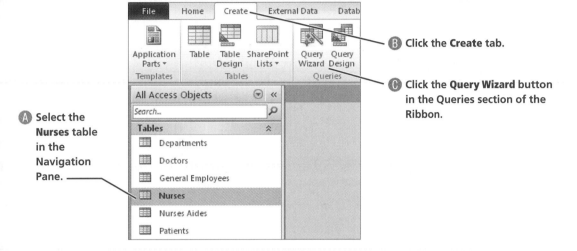

Ⓐ Select the **Nurses** table in the Navigation Pane.

Ⓑ Click the **Create** tab.

Ⓒ Click the **Query Wizard** button in the Queries section of the Ribbon.

3. Follow these steps to select the query type:

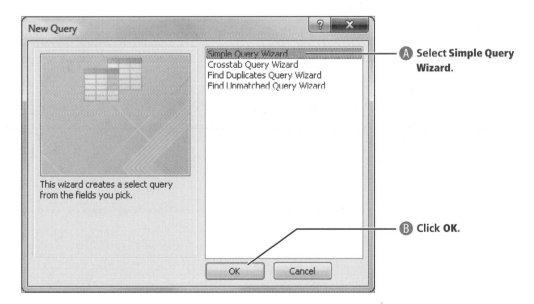

Ⓐ Select **Simple Query Wizard**.

Ⓑ Click **OK**.

4. Follow these steps to move selected fields to the query:

A Ensure that the **table name** appears in the Tables/Queries box.

B Select the **NrFirstName** field in the Available Fields list.

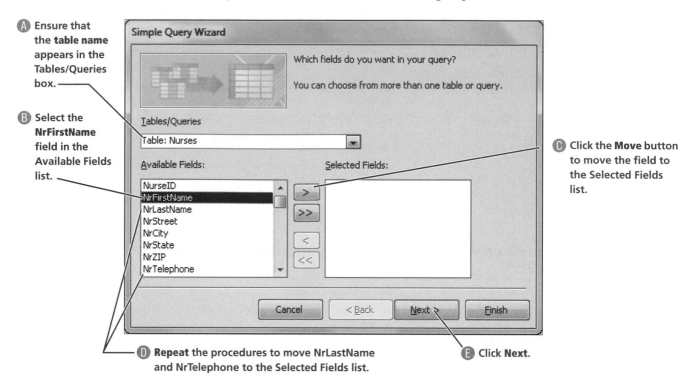

C Click the **Move** button to move the field to the Selected Fields list.

D **Repeat** the procedures to move NrLastName and NrTelephone to the Selected Fields list.

E Click **Next**.

5. Follow these steps to complete the query:

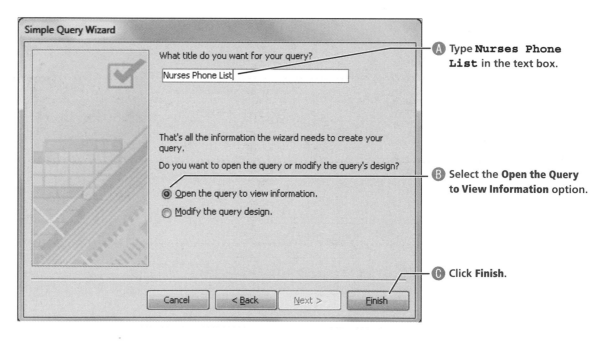

A Type **Nurses Phone List** in the text box.

B Select the **Open the Query to View Information** option.

C Click **Finish**.

6. **Review** the query results datasheet and then **close** ☒ the query.

Creating a Select Query Using Query Design

Video Lesson labyrinthelab.com/videos

The query you created in Develop Your Skills 4.1.1 simply reported the data contained in the selected fields without regard to limiting the records Access listed. When databases grow to contain voluminous records, it is often necessary to select specific records from a database by setting criteria. Using Query Design view, you will be able to take advantage of features that allow you to:

- Select fields from multiple tables
- Set criteria to locate records based on data contained in one or more fields
- Calculate totals
- Show fields containing criteria that are hidden in the query results datasheet

Identifying Features of the Query Design Grid

When you use Query Design, a grid displays that enables you to add multiple tables to the query and place fields from each table into the display grid. You can place the fields in the order in which you want them to appear in the query results datasheet and change the arrangement as necessary. In addition, the query design grid contains elements that enable you to set criteria, sort data in the query results, and so forth.

Tables containing fields to be included in the query appear in the upper pane of the Query Design window.

Fields to include in the query appear in the first row of the grid in the bottom pane.

Additional elements enable you to set Criteria, Sort data, and so forth.

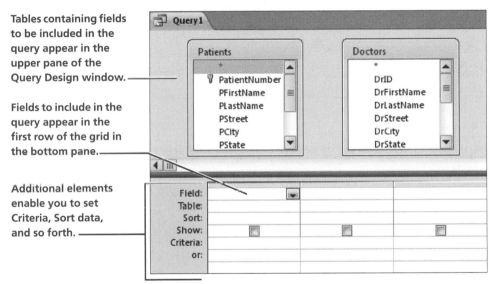

The Query Design Grid

Adding Fields to the Query Design Grid

Access offers a variety of different techniques for adding fields to the query grid. These include:

- Double-clicking a field name to add the field to the next available column of the query design grid
- Dragging a field to the next column in the grid
- Clicking the Field row of a column in the query grid and selecting the field from the drop-down list
- Double-clicking the asterisk (*) that appears at the top of the field list to add all fields to the grid

 When you use the asterisk to add all fields to the grid, Access places the table name in the Field row, but when you run the query, each field appears in a separate column of the query results datasheet.

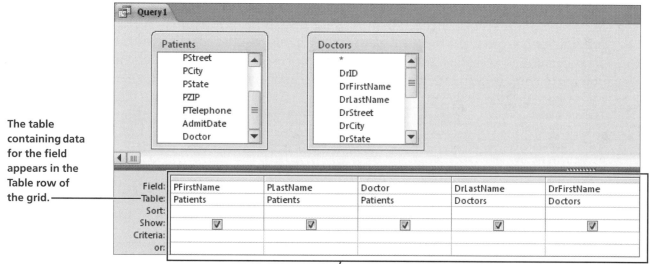

The table containing data for the field appears in the Table row of the grid.

Each field appears in a separate column.

Rearranging Fields in the Query Design Grid

Regardless of whether the datasheet displays table data or query results data, you can rearrange the columns by dragging them and dropping them in a new position. You can also drag a column in a query grid to reposition it, when necessary. Click the narrow gray bar button that appears above a column in the query grid, and then point to the top edge of the selected column and drag it to a new position.

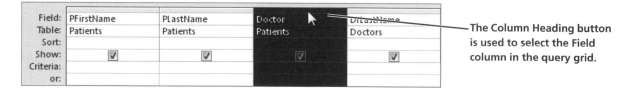

The Column Heading button is used to select the Field column in the query grid.

Task	Procedure
Create a query using query design	■ Choose Create→Queries→Query Design 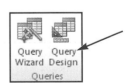 on the Ribbon.
Display query design from the query Datasheet View	■ Choose Home→Views→View on the Ribbon. *or* ■ Click the Views menu ▼ and select Design View. *or* ■ Right-click the query tab and select Design View from the shortcut menu.
Add fields to a query grid	■ Double-click a field name in the table field list. *or* ■ Drag a field from the table field list to a column of the query grid. *or* ■ Double-click the asterisk in the table field list to add all fields from the table to the query grid. *or* ■ Click Field row in the query grid and select the field from the drop-down list.
Add criteria to a query grid	■ Type criteria into the Criteria row for the field that should contain the value.
Save a query	■ Create the query and click Save. ■ Type a name for the query and click OK.
Run a query	■ Double-click a query name in the Navigation Pane. *or* ■ Create the query and display the query in Design View. ■ Choose Design→Results→Run on the Ribbon.

DEVELOP YOUR SKILLS 4.1.2

Create a Query Using Query Design

You have already created a telephone list for the Nurses and now need one for the Doctors. In this exercise, you will create a query containing fields from the Doctors table in the Raritan Clinic East Queries database, rearrange the columns in the query grid, and sort the query results list.

1. **Open** your Raritan Clinic East Queries database, if it is closed, and then choose **Create→Queries→Query Design** on the Ribbon to display the Query Design Grid.
   Access creates a new query, displays the query grid, and opens a list of tables contained in the database so that you can choose the tables you want to include in the query.

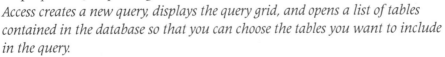

2. Follow these steps to add the Doctors table to the query:

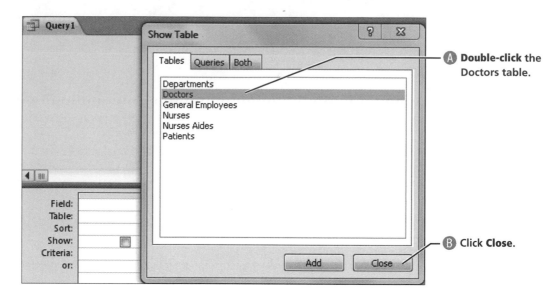

A **Double-click** the Doctors table.

B Click **Close**.

Notice that the table name appears in the field list title bar.

3. Follow these steps to add fields to the query grid:

A **Double-click** DrFirstName to add it to the query grid first column.

B **Double-click** DrLastName to add it to the query grid second column.

C **Double-click** the DrTelephone to add it to the query grid third column.

D **Double-click** the DrCellPhone to add it to the query grid fourth column.

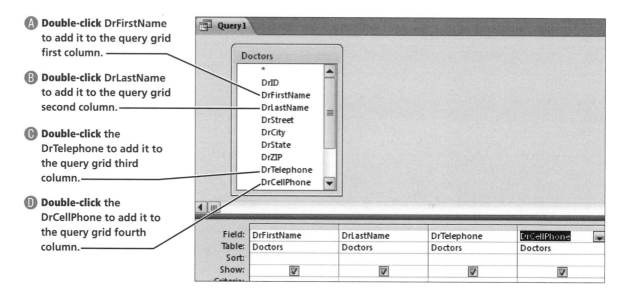

4. Follow these steps to save and then run the query:

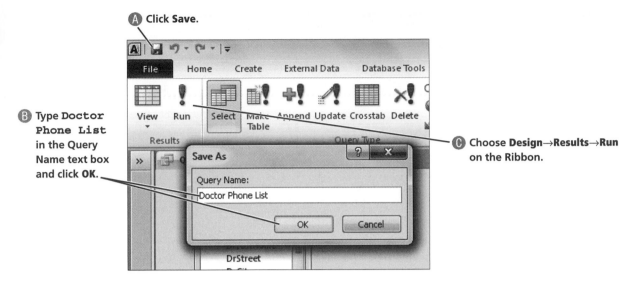

Ⓐ Click **Save**.

Ⓑ Type **Doctor Phone List** in the Query Name text box and click **OK**.

Ⓒ Choose **Design→Results→Run** on the Ribbon.

Access runs the query and displays two columns of data for all records in the database tables.

5. **Press** Tab to advance to the Last Name field column and then choose **Home→Sort & Filter→Ascending** to sort the list alphabetically by last name.

6. Choose **Home→Views→View** on the ribbon to switch to Design view.

7. Follow these steps to move the DrLastName field to the left of DrFirstName:

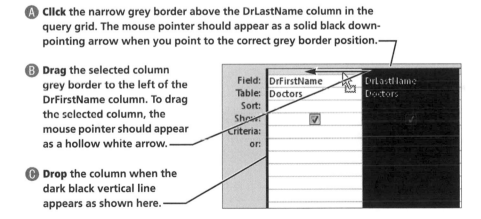

Ⓐ **Click** the narrow grey border above the DrLastName column in the query grid. The mouse pointer should appear as a solid black down-pointing arrow when you point to the correct grey border position.

Ⓑ **Drag** the selected column grey border to the left of the DrFirstName column. To drag the selected column, the mouse pointer should appear as a hollow white arrow.

Ⓒ **Drop** the column when the dark black vertical line appears as shown here.

8. Choose **Design→Results→Run** to run the query again.

9. **Close** the query, **saving** changes when prompted.

Designing a Query Using Multiple Tables

Video Lesson labyrinthelab.com/videos

Until now, all the datasheets you have seen have displayed data from only one table. There will be times when you want to view data that is contained in different tables within or linked to the same database. Queries make displaying data from multiple tables possible.

Choosing Fields to Include in a Query

When you build a query, you select only those fields that you want to display in the query results datasheet—leaving out those fields that have no impact on the data you want to view or that are confidential. For example, if you were responsible for maintaining a list of FBI agents, would you want everyone with access to the database to know the addresses and phone numbers of all agents? By selecting only specific fields of data in database tables and displaying those fields in a query, you can use the query as the basis for creating a report or a form, thus protecting the confidential data. When the data you want to display in a query results datasheet appears in different tables in the database, you simply add those tables to the query design grid to make fields from the tables available.

Selecting a Field Appearing in Multiple Tables

Many times, as you work with table field lists, you will use tables containing the same field names and wonder which field you should add to a query. There are various ways to determine which field list to use for a field:

- Review the table data for the tables containing the same field name. In many cases, you will be able to determine which table field to use based on the query results you want.

- Identify the table for which a field is the primary key. In many cases, the primary key will enable you to pull other data contained in the table. For example, if you want to use the Customer Number field to access a customer name, you would use the Customer Number field from the table that also contains the customer name.

DrID is the primary key field in the Doctors table.

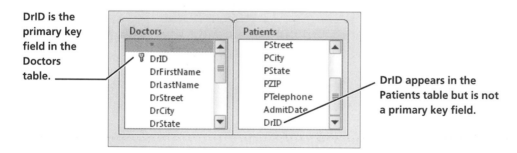

DrID appears in the Patients table but is not a primary key field.

Create a Multi-Table Query

In this exercise, you will create a multi-table query using Query Design View that displays patient names from the Patients table and their doctors' names from the Doctors table.

Before You Begin: Your Raritan Clinic East Queries database should be open.

1. Choose **Create→Queries→Query Design** on the Ribbon.

2. **Double-click** the following table names in the Show Table dialog box to add the table field lists to the upper pane of the query: Patients and Doctors.

3. **Close** the Show Table dialog box, and then follow these steps to add fields to the query grid:

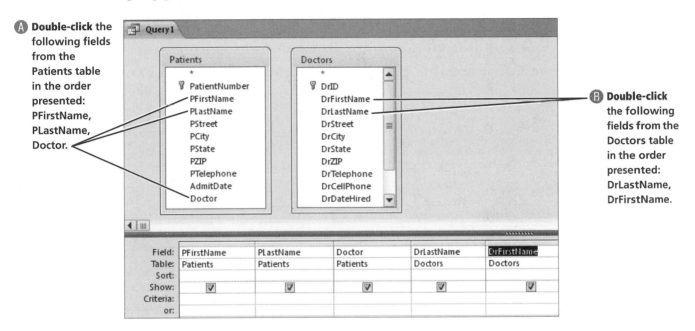

Ⓐ **Double-click** the following fields from the Patients table in the order presented: PFirstName, PLastName, Doctor.

Ⓑ **Double-click** the following fields from the Doctors table in the order presented: DrLastName, DrFirstName.

The fields should appear in the query grid in the order shown in the figure.

4. **Save** the query using the query name **Patients & Doctors**.

5. Choose **Design→Results→Run** on the Ribbon to display the query results.

6. **Close** the query results datasheet.

Video Lesson   labyrinthelab.com/videos

As you begin working with large databases that contain hundreds of thousands of records, you experience the power behind queries that enables you to specify *criteria*—conditions that data must meet. When you run the query, Access will list only those records containing data that meet the criteria. This is the feature used by sportscasters, telephone order clerks, and others who need data instantly.

Adding Criteria to a Query

The conditions and comparison format used in queries to limit or control the number of records Access finds resemble the criteria you set when you filter tables by form. The same comparison operators ($<$, $>$, $=$, $>=$, $<=$, $<>$) used in setting validation rules help define criteria in queries.Setting criteria limits the number of records displayed in a query results datasheet to only those records with values in the selected field columns that meet the criteria. In addition, the following comparison and logical criteria can be used to limit data returned in queries:

Criteria Expression	Description
> 123	For a numeric data field, returns records for values greater than 123.
< 100.45	For a currency data field, values less than 100.45.
>= Smith	For a text data field, all values from Smith through the end of the alphabet.
Between 2/2/1999 And 12/1/1999	For date data field, dates from February 2, 1999 through December 1, 1999.
Not Smith	For a text data field, all records for values except Smith.
Not 2	For numeric data field, all values except those equal to 2.
Not T*	For text data field, all values that don't start with the letter T.
In("Canada", "UK")	For a text data field, records containing the values Canada or UK in the criteria field.
"London" Or "Hedge End"	For a text data field, orders shipped to London or Hedge End.
Date()	For a date data field, values for today's date.
Between Date( ) And DateAdd ("M", 3, Date( ))	For a date data field, values required between today's date and three months from today's date.
< Date( ) – 30	For a date data field, values 30 days prior to the current date.

Hiding Columns in the Query Results Datasheet

Sometimes you will need to enter criteria in a field contained in a query grid and display values from a different field. The Show checkbox in the query grid enables you to hide or show fields in the query results datasheet by simply checking or clearing the check in the Show box.

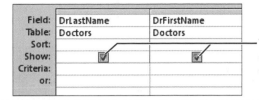

The Show box appears for each field in the query grid so that you can check those you want to display in the query results datasheet.

Saving Queries with Criteria

When you add criteria to a query to locate specific records in the database, Access recognizes the criteria as a change in the query design. As a result, when you close the query, Access prompts you to save it. Saving the query saves the criteria as part of the query. Sometimes, when you find yourself setting the same criteria for a query time and time again, you may want to save the query with the criteria. Many times, however, you will want to set different criteria each time you run the query. In those cases, you would want to respond to the save prompt by choosing No.

DEVELOP YOUR SKILLS 4.2.1
Add Criteria and Run a Query

In this exercise, you will add criteria to the query grid and run the query.

1. **Open** the Navigation Pane and **double-click** the Patients & Doctors query to run the query.

2. Choose **Home→Views→View** on the Ribbon to display Query Design View.

3. Follow these steps to add criteria to the query grid:

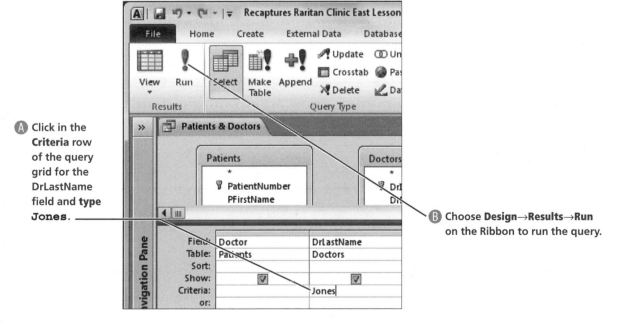

Ⓐ Click in the **Criteria** row of the query grid for the **DrLastName** field and **type Jones**.

Ⓑ Choose **Design→Results→Run** on the Ribbon to run the query.

Access runs the query and searches the database for all Patients for Dr. Jones.

4. Choose **Design→Views→View** to return to Design View and then follow these steps to remove a column from display:

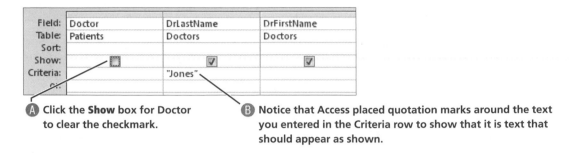

Ⓐ Click the **Show** box for Doctor to clear the checkmark.

Ⓑ Notice that Access placed quotation marks around the text you entered in the Criteria row to show that it is text that should appear as shown.

5. Choose **Design→Results→Run** and review the results datasheet.

6. **Close** the query. Choose **No** when prompted to save changes to the query.
Saving changes to the query now saves the new field as part of the query. It also saves the criteria as part of the query. Because you plan to use the query to set criteria to display records for other patients, you will need to remove the existing criteria before running it for another patient.

Using Wildcards

Video Lesson   labyrinthelab.com/videos

The two most frequent wildcards with which you may already be familiar are the asterisk (*) and the question mark (?). There are four additional wildcards available. Each of the wildcards is described in the following Quick Reference table.

QUICK REFERENCE	DEFINING WILDCARD SYMBOLS
Symbol	**Description of Use**
An asterisk (*)	Substitutes for a group of characters that appears at the position of the asterisk
	Example: If you type **R*** in the last name column of a query grid, Access will locate all names beginning with *R* regardless of how many characters make up the name—*Rogers, Rich,* and *Rovarino* would all appear in the results datasheet.
A question mark (?)	Substitutes for a single character that might appear at the position of the question mark
	Example: If you type **m?s** in the criteria row for a column, Access will locate records containing values such as *mrs, ms, mbs,* and so forth.
Open/close brackets [ ]	Matches text or individual characters placed within the brackets individually.
	Example: If you type ca[rt], Access will find cat and car but not cab or cad, etc.
Exclamation point (!)	Matches any character within the brackets *except* those characters that follow the !.
	Example: If you type ca[!rt], Access will find cab, cad, cam, etc., but *not* cat or car.
Hyphen (-)	Matches characters at the wildcard position that fall within a range of ascending values.
	Example: If you type ca[a-r], Access finds cab, cad, cam, car, etc., but *not* cat or cay.
Number sign (#)	Locates any numeric digit at the position of the #.
	Example: If you type #10, Access locates 010, 110, 210, etc.

Examples of query criteria are shown in the following figure.

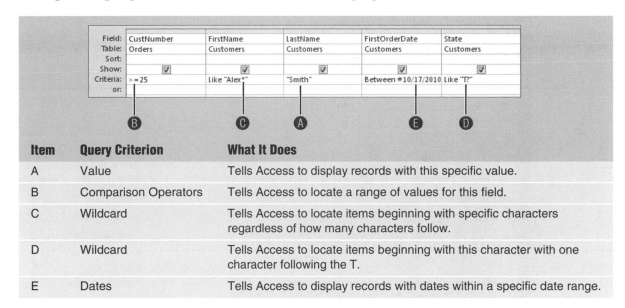

Item	Query Criterion	What It Does
A	Value	Tells Access to display records with this specific value.
B	Comparison Operators	Tells Access to locate a range of values for this field.
C	Wildcard	Tells Access to locate items beginning with specific characters regardless of how many characters follow.
D	Wildcard	Tells Access to locate items beginning with this character with one character following the T.
E	Dates	Tells Access to display records with dates within a specific date range.

Setting AND and OR Criteria

In some cases, as you query a database, you need to select records that meet multiple criteria. Access uses two basic criteria conditions that apply to setting multiple criteria—AND and OR. The basic principles for determining whether to use AND or OR criteria in queries are as follows:

QUICK REFERENCE	USING *AND* AND *OR* CRITERIA
Criterion Type	**Description**
AND	Use to select records that meet all criteria set in all query grid fields. For example, you might set AND criteria to locate customers from a specific city within a state by typing the city name in the City field on the query grid and the state in the State field on the grid.
OR	Use to select records meeting one condition or another condition whether the criteria are set for the same field or different fields. For example, you could set OR criteria to locate customers from two different states. By setting OR criteria, Access displays all records containing one state *or* the other state in the State field.

Positioning Multiple Criteria in the Query Grid

In the query grid, AND criteria all appear on the *Criteria* row even when criteria are set for different fields. The word *And* appears between values in the same field. When you set OR criteria, the first criterion is entered on the *Criteria* row of the grid while other criteria appear on the *or* row of the grid.

Example – AND Criteria

Setting criteria for two different fields on the *Criteria* row creates an AND condition. With this type of criterion, Access locates only those records for people whose last name is Ballard and whose doctor is Dr. Jones (5004). People whose last name is Ballard who have a different doctor will not appear when you run the query.

The criteria are on the same row.

Example – OR Criteria

Using the same values, setting 5004 on the *or* row of the query grid tells Access to look for all patients named Ballard in the table or anyone whose doctor is Dr. Jones (5004). Patients who have other doctors will be shown if their last name is Ballard,

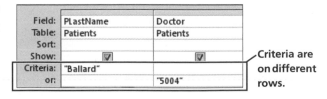

and Dr. Jones' patients will be shown regardless of their last name.

Using AND and OR Criteria

Sometimes setting AND and OR criteria seems to operate backwards. For example, if you want to locate all records for patients from TX or LA, you use an OR condition. The query results shows more listings than if you type only one value in the grid—all records for patients from both TX and LA. If you consider that there are no records that contain both TX and LA in the *State* field, it begins to make sense.

DEVELOP YOUR SKILLS 4.2.2

Use Wildcards and Multiple Criteria in Queries

In this exercise, you will set multiple criteria in queries and also use wildcards to locate variable data in records in the Raritan Clinic East Queries database.

1. **Right-click** the Patients & Doctors query in the Navigation pane and choose **Design View**.

2. Follow these steps to set Or criterion using two values for two fields:

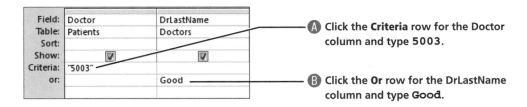

These criteria will locate all records for doctor #5003 as well as all records for Dr. Good.

3. Choose **Design→Results→Run** ![run icon] on the Ribbon to run the query.

4. Click the **Last Name** column and then click the **Ascending** button on the Ribbon.

5. Review the query results datasheet:

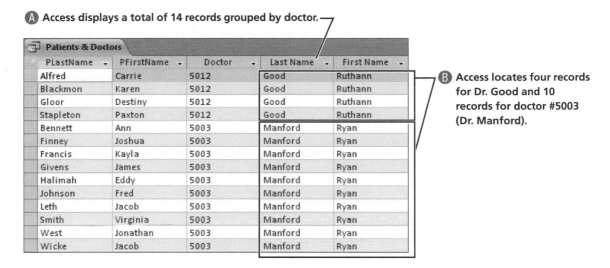

Ⓐ Access displays a total of 14 records grouped by doctor.

Ⓑ Access locates four records for Dr. Good and 10 records for doctor #5003 (Dr. Manford).

6. Choose **Home→Views→View** 🖊 on the Ribbon to return to Query Design View.

7. **Clear** the criteria in the Or row for DrLastName and then type **Francis** in the Or row for PLastName.

8. Choose **Design→Results→Run** ❗ on the Ribbon to run the query.
   Access locates 11 records—one for a patient with the last name of Francis and ten for Dr. Manford. Do you see the record for Dr. Manford's patient with the last name of Francis?

9. Choose **Home→Views→View** 🖊 on the Ribbon to return to Query Design View.

Use Wildcards

10. **Clear** all criteria from the Criteria and Or rows and then follow these steps to set different criteria:

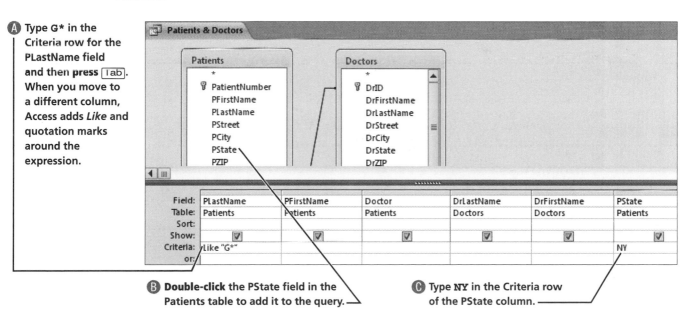

Ⓐ Type **G*** in the Criteria row for the PLastName field and then **press** ⎀Tab⎀. When you move to a different column, Access adds *Like* and quotation marks around the expression.

Ⓑ **Double-click** the PState field in the Patients table to add it to the query.

Ⓒ Type **NY** in the Criteria row of the PState column.

This criteria locates all patients from NY whose last name begins with G, regardless of what other characters might be part of the last name.

11. Choose **Design→Results→Run** on the Ribbon to run the query.
Access locates 1 record—for the NY patient whose last name begins with G.

12. **Close** ☒ the query without saving changes. Choose **No** when prompted to save changes.
Saving changes at this point would store the criteria with the query.

Entering Date Criteria

Video Lesson labyrinthelab.com/videos

The "plain English" approach to entering criteria in Access queries can make comparing date values more logical. You can set date criteria to determine age, expired licenses, and so forth. Access acknowledges the same comparison criteria for performing date comparisons that it does for locating other types of data—regardless of the format used to enter dates.

SAMPLES OF DATE CRITERIA	
Criterion	**Locates**
11/22/2006	Locates records containing the specific date
<22-Nov-2006	Locates records containing dates that occur before the specific date—regardless of how the date is typed
>11/22/06	Locates records containing dates that occur after the specific date
<=#11/22/06#	Locates records containing dates on or before the specific date; the # signs that appear before and after the date help Access identify the data between them as a date
Between 11/22/06 and 11/22/08	Locates records containing dates after the first date and before the second date

DEVELOP YOUR SKILLS 4.2.3
Use Date Criteria in Queries

A list of new admissions is printed each day and given to the information desk for easy reference when answering phone calls. In this exercise, you will create a new query to set criteria for locating records using date values.

1. Choose **Create→Queries→Query Design** 🖼.

2. **Double-click** the Patients table and then the Doctors table in the Add Table dialog box to add the table field lists to the query and **close** the Show Table dialog box.

3. **Double-click** each of the following fields in the Patients table to add the fields to the query grid: PFirstName, PLastName, AdmitDate.

4. **Double-click** the *DrLastName* field in the Doctors table to add the field to the query grid.

5. Click the **Save** 💾 button, type **Daily Admissions** in the Query Name field, and then click **OK** to save the query.

6. Type **January 15, 2010** into the *Criteria* row for the AdmitDate field column.
Regardless of whether you type the date as entered here or as 01/15/10 or 1-15-2010, Access formats the date after you enter it so that it appears as #1/15/2010#.

7. Choose **Design→Results→Run** on the Ribbon to run the query.
   Access locates two records for patients admitted on January 15, 2010.

8. **Close** the query, without saving changes when prompted.

4.3 Sorting a Query and Limiting Results

Video Lesson   labyrinthelab.com/videos

The sorting techniques you may already know can also be used to sort query results datasheets in ascending or descending order after you run the query. In addition, the query grid contains a *Sort* row that you can set so that Access sorts data in the query results datasheet as it runs the query. The same sort orders—ascending and descending—are available in the query grid Sort listings. Sorting data as you run the query ensures consistency in data organization to make locating data in the query results datasheet more efficient. When you work with large volumes of data, limiting the number of records shown in the query results datasheet can also be helpful. Access contains tools that enable you to limit the number of records displayed.

Setting a Query Sort Order

Because the sort order for a query varies according to the information you want to retrieve, creating a copy of a query and saving each query using a different sort order can also be beneficial. In addition, there will be times when you want to sort data on two fields so that when the data in one field (such as *LastName* or *State*) is the same, Access looks at the second field (such as *FirstName* or *City*) to sort. When two fields are set as sort fields, Access sorts the fields left to right as they appear in the query grid. The first field found with a sort order identified is the primary sort field; the next field containing a sort order is the secondary sort field. There is no need to arrange the columns in the query grid side by side to sort multiple fields.

The Sort row of the query grid.——

—Sort orders available.

 Multi-valued lookup fields cannot be used as sort fields.

Limiting Number of Results Displayed

Running queries on large databases containing many tables and hundreds of thousands of records often returns such a large number of results when you run a query that it can be challenging to filter out the data records you were looking for. Limiting the number of records Access displays when you run a query can be beneficial, especially when combined with sorting features.

For example, if you set up a query to sort the query results in descending order and then limit the number of items displayed to ten, you would, if effect, have a list of the top ten items in the table or tables being queried.

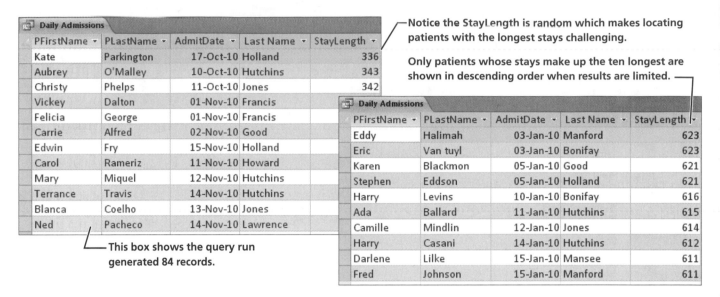

Notice the StayLength is random which makes locating patients with the longest stays challenging.

Only patients whose stays make up the ten longest are shown in descending order when results are limited.

Daily Admissions

PFirstName	PLastName	AdmitDate	Last Name	StayLength
Kate	Parkington	17-Oct-10	Holland	336
Aubrey	O'Malley	10-Oct-10	Hutchins	343
Christy	Phelps	11-Oct-10	Jones	342
Vickey	Dalton	01-Nov-10	Francis	
Felicia	George	01-Nov-10	Francis	
Carrie	Alfred	02-Nov-10	Good	
Edwin	Fry	15-Nov-10	Holland	
Carol	Rameriz	11-Nov-10	Howard	
Mary	Miquel	12-Nov-10	Hutchins	
Terrance	Travis	14-Nov-10	Hutchins	
Blanca	Coelho	13-Nov-10	Jones	
Ned	Pacheco	14-Nov-10	Lawrence	

This box shows the query run generated 84 records.

Daily Admissions

PFirstName	PLastName	AdmitDate	Last Name	StayLength
Eddy	Halimah	03-Jan-10	Manford	623
Eric	Van tuyl	03-Jan-10	Bonifay	623
Karen	Blackmon	05-Jan-10	Good	621
Stephen	Eddson	05-Jan-10	Holland	621
Harry	Levins	10-Jan-10	Bonifay	616
Ada	Ballard	11-Jan-10	Hutchins	615
Camille	Mindlin	12-Jan-10	Jones	614
Harry	Casani	14-Jan-10	Hutchins	612
Darlene	Lilke	15-Jan-10	Mansee	611
Fred	Johnson	15-Jan-10	Manford	611

The Return feature on the Query Design tab of the Ribbon enables you to set the number of records to be returned. The default setting for this feature is *All*.

QUICK REFERENCE	SETTING A QUERY SORT ORDER
Task	**Procedure**
Set a sort order	<ul><li>Display the query in Query Design View.</li><li>Click the Sort row of the query grid for the field on which you want to sort.</li><li>Select the appropriate sort order for the field.</li></ul>
Set sort orders for multiple fields	<ul><li>Display the query in Query Design View and arrange the fields left to right in the order in which you want Access to sort.</li><li>Click the Sort row of the query grid for the field on which you want to sort.</li><li>Select the appropriate sort order for the field.</li><li>Repeat these steps for each additional field that you want to sort.</li></ul>
Limit the number of records returned	<ul><li>Display the query in Query Design View.</li><li>Choose Design→Query Setup→Return menu and select the number of records you want to view.</li></ul>

Set a Query Sort Order

In this exercise, you will set a sort order in the query grid to sort the Daily Admissions results in descending order and limit the results to display the last ten admissions.

Before You Begin: The Raritan Clinic East Queries database should be open.

1. **Right-click** the Daily Admissions query and select **Design View** to open the query in Query Design View.

2. Follow these steps to set a sort order in the query grid:

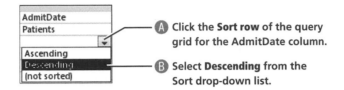

Ⓐ Click the **Sort row** of the query grid for the AdmitDate column.

Ⓑ Select **Descending** from the Sort drop-down list.

3. Choose **Design→Query Setup→Return** text box on the Ribbon and type **10**.

4. Choose **Design→Results→Run** [!] on the Ribbon to run the query.
   Access displays only the records for the last ten admissions to the clinic.

5. **Close** the query, choosing **No** when prompted to save changes to the query.
   If you save changes after setting the number of records to display, Access saves that number as part of the query. In this case, you do not want to display only ten records each time you run the query.

4.4 Performing Calculations in Queries

Video Lesson labyrinthelab.com/videos

So far, the activities in this lesson have introduced the basics of creating, running, sorting, and selecting records based on criteria. As you developed the queries, you used fields available in field lists from database tables. Access also contains features that enable you to use the query grid to create a *calculated field*—a field that contains no data in a table but uses data in other fields to obtain its value.

A calculated field:

- Creates a new field in the query that can be used in a form or report
- Has a name and can be formatted with properties as a regular field
- Enables you to combine values in two text fields, such as FirstName and LastName, into one field
- Can be used to perform mathematical operations such as add, multiply, etc.
- Updates and recalculates each time you run the query

Queries, forms, tables, and reports can contain calculated fields. As a result, it is a good idea to identify calculated fields as you design a database and mark them as calculated fields so that you include in database tables all the fields used in the calculated fields.

Identifying Parts of a Calculated Field

The structure of a calculated field includes a field name and expression elements that tell Access which fields, operators, and punctuation marks to use to create the field. Each calculated field contains the following elements:

ELEMENTS OF CALCULATED FIELDS	
Element	**Description**
Calculated field name	■ The unique name you assign to the field, followed by a colon to separate the field name from the expression.
Field names from existing tables	■ The field containing the data used in the calculation. If field names from different tables appear in the calculated field, Access adds the table name containing the field. Field names appear in brackets [ ].
Arithmetic or comparison operators	■ +, -, /, *, =, >, <, and so forth to compare values or perform mathematical operations. ■ The ampersand (&) is used to join text values from multiple fields such as FirstName & LastName. Required spaces appear within quotation marks (" ").

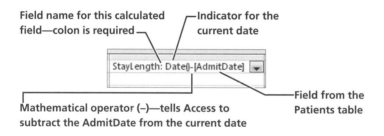

Field name for this calculated field—colon is required

Indicator for the current date

StayLength: Date()-[AdmitDate]

Mathematical operator (–)—tells Access to subtract the AdmitDate from the current date

Field from the Patients table

Identifying Order of Calculations

As you may have learned during your study of math or other computer programs that perform calculations (such as Excel), there is a distinct order used to perform mathematical calculations. Access calculates mathematical operations left to right across a formula by applying the rules of order for calculating. The standard order for performing mathematical operations is often abbreviated *PEMDAS* (you may have learned the phrase *Please excuse my dear Aunt Sally,* a phrase often taught in elementary schools to teach order of operations). The initials represent the order of mathematical operations Access uses, as described in the following Quick Reference table.

$$(2+2) * 3^2 - 6/2 = 33$$

Item	Calculation	Description
A	**P**arentheses	Calculations enclosed in parentheses are performed first.
B	**E**xponentials	Calculations "raised to the power of", such as squared or cubed, are performed next. Exponents appear as raised numbers, such as in x^2.
C	**M**ultiplication/**D**ivision	Multiplication and division are equal in calculation order and are calculated left to right, after calculations on parentheses and exponentials.
D	**A**ddition/**S**ubtraction	Addition and subtraction are equal in calculation order and are calculated last, left to right across a formula.

Calculating Dates

In addition to performing simple calculations involving dates, Access provides alternative ways to use dates in calculated fields. You can use these expressions to calculate age, number of years in business, and so forth. Samples of dates used in calculated fields are shown in the following Quick Reference table.

Sample Field	Returns
CurrentDate: =Date() or CurrentDate: Now()	Displays the current date in the *mm-dd-yyyy* format, where *mm* is the month, *dd* is the day, and *yyyy* is the year.
OrderProcessing: DateDiff("d", [OrderDate], [ShippedDate])	Displays the number of days (d) between the value in the OrderDate field and the ShippedDate field.
(Now()-[DOB])/365	Subtracts the value in the DOB (date of birth) field from the current date and divides the difference by 365 to display the calculated value in years.

Creating and Formatting a Calculated Field

Each calculated field stored in a query appears in a separate column in the query grid. You can type the calculated field into the Field row of the column or create one using tools on the Ribbon in the Query Design View to access the expression builder used to build a calculated field. Other tools on the Ribbon enable you to access field properties for fields used in queries.

Setting Calculated Field Properties

When you create tables in Access, you are able to set field properties—captions, input masks, default values, format, and so forth. Calculated fields often need to be formatted using field properties. To assign field properties to calculated fields, you use the Property Sheet.

FROM THE KEYBOARD

Alt+Enter to open the Property Sheet
F4 to open the Property Sheet

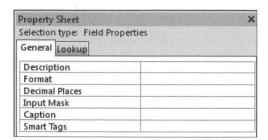

The Property Sheet for formatting query fields.

DEVELOP YOUR SKILLS 4.4.1

Create and Format a Calculated Field

In this exercise, you will create a calculated field for a query in your Raritan Clinic East Queries database.

Before You Begin: The Raritan Clinic East Queries database should be open.

1. **Right-click** the Daily Admissions query in the Navigation pane and choose **Design View**.

2. Follow these steps to create a calculated field that calculates the number of days each patient has been in the clinic.

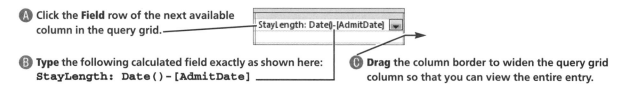

Ⓐ Click the **Field** row of the next available column in the query grid.

Ⓑ **Type** the following calculated field exactly as shown here: **StayLength: Date()-[AdmitDate]**

Ⓒ **Drag** the column border to widen the query grid column so that you can view the entire entry.

3. **Run** the query.

   Access displays the number of days each patient has been in the clinic. Because the current date varies for each student completing this activity, the dates will vary from negative dates to positive dates and may seem as if they are too large. If you were to create such a calculated field in an actively running database, the length of each patient's stay would be much more reasonable. If your query calculated incorrectly, check the field for typographical errors.

4. **Save** changes to the query and **close** it.

Using a Function in a Query Expression

Video Lesson   labyrinthelab.com/videos

If you have worked with Microsoft Excel, you are most likely familiar with the types of functions that provide Excel with its calculating power. In Access, you have many of the same types of functions available for performing specific calculations, such as finding the minimum, maximum, and average values, and counting the number of entries in a datasheet. These are known as *aggregate functions* and are built into Access to calculate totals for field values. You can use these functions in queries, forms, and reports to aid in reporting database data.

Adding Functions to the Query Grid

When you want to add functions for totaling, finding averages or similar values based on data contained in database tables, you must first display the Totals row on the query grid. From the totals row, you choose the function you want to calculate for a specified field—using a separate column for each function. For example, if you want to find three different values for the same

---

field—minimum, maximum, and average—you would add the field to the query grid three times—once for each function.

When you first display the Totals row in the query grid, Access places the *Group By* command in the total row for each column. You can use the Group By function to calculate values by each different value in the field. For example, if you added the State field to the grid, you could group by the State field and Access would calculate averages for each state separately.

Total row in the query grid.

Group by appears in most columns.

Field:	DrLastName	MinStayLength: Date(	AvgStayLength: Date(	MaxStayLength: Date(
Table:	Doctors			
Total:	Group By	Group By	Group By	Group By
Sort:				
Show:	☑	☑	☑	☑
Criteria:				

Creating Aliases in Query Fields

Calculated fields are designed to calculate values for summarizing data. As a result, values in calculated fields are not stored in database tables. When you want to use calculated fields for displaying multiple function values in a query, you copy the calculated field to additional columns of the query grid. Then you have to assign a different field name to each additional function value you want to locate.

Alias Example

Suppose you create a calculated field named TotalWages that calculates the weekly wages for each employee. It is conceivable that you may want to find the average, minimum, and maximum values for the calculated field among all employees. When you copy the calculated expression to two additional columns in the query grid, you would need to change the name of the calculated field—the part of the expression that appears before the colon—for each additional instance of the expression. When the same expression is assigned several different field names, the additional field names are referred to as *aliases*.

⌐**Original calculated field name finds the Minimum value.**

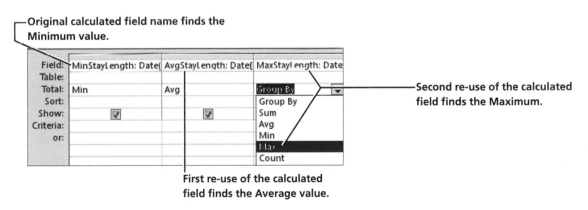

Field:	MinStayLength: Date(	AvgStayLength: Date(	MaxStayLength: Date
Table:			
Total:	Min	Avg	Group By
Sort:			Group By
Show:	☑	☑	Sum
Criteria:			Avg
or:			Min
			Max
			Count

Second re-use of the calculated field finds the Maximum.

First re-use of the calculated field finds the Average value.

Identifying Function Types

Simple aggregate functions allow you to count the number of entries in a field, locate the maximum or minimum values in a field, total the values of a group of records, and find the average value from a group of values. Access contains additional functions that enable you to calculate the standard deviation and variance of values. It is also important to know that Access limits or restricts the use of these functions to specific data field types. Some of the more commonly used aggregate functions are identified in the following table.

AGGREGATE FUNCTION TYPES

Function	Description	Valid Field Data Types
Sum	Totals values in a field.	Number, Currency
Avg	Averages values in a field.	Number, Date/Time, Currency
Min	Identifies lowest value in a field.	Text, Number, Date/Time, Currency
Max	Identifies highest value in a field.	Text, Number, Date/Time, Currency
Count	Counts the number of values in a field, not counting (blank) values.	All types except multi-value lists
StDev	Calculates standard deviation of the values in a field.	Number, Currency
Var	Calculates variance of the values in a field.	Number, Currency
First	Locates the first record in the group on which you are performing calculations in chronological order without sorting.	All data types
Last	Locates the last record in the group on which you are performing calculations in chronological order without sorting.	All data types

DEVELOP YOUR SKILLS 4.4.2
Use Functions in Queries

In this exercise, you will create a query by saving an existing query as a new query. Then you will edit the new query so that it displays the query design you need and use functions to identify minimum, maximum, averages, and counts of records for a query in your Raritan Clinic East Queries database.

Before You Begin: The Raritan Clinic East Queries database should be open.

1. **Right-click** the Daily Admissions query in the Navigation pane and choose **Copy**.

2. **Right-click** the Daily Admissions query again, choose Paste, type **Daily Admissions Summary** as the new query name, and then click **OK**.

3. Open the Daily Admissions Summary query in Design View and then follow these steps to remove unnecessary fields from the query grid:

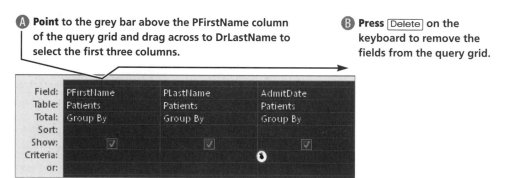

Ⓐ **Point** to the grey bar above the PFirstName column of the query grid and drag across to DrLastName to select the first three columns.

Ⓑ **Press** Delete on the keyboard to remove the fields from the query grid.

4. Follow these steps to copy and paste the StayLength calculated field to two additional columns in the query grid:

(A) **Right-click** the grey bar at the top of the StayLength calculated field to select the column and then choose Copy.

(B) **Right-click** the grey bar at the top of the first blank column in the query grid and choose Paste to paste the calculated field.

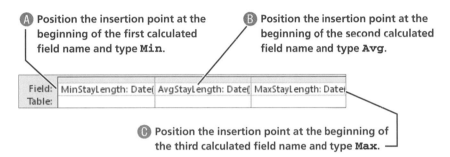

(C) **Repeat** the procedure outlined in Step B to paste the calculated field in the next column.

You should now have three columns in the query grid that contain the calculated field for StayLength. You need to change the field name for each of the calculated fields.

5. Follow these steps to change the field name for the calculated fields:

(A) **Position** the insertion point at the beginning of the first calculated field name and type **Min**.

(B) **Position** the insertion point at the beginning of the second calculated field name and type **Avg**.

Field:	MinStayLength: Date(	AvgStayLength: Date(	MaxStayLength: Date(
Table:			

(C) **Position** the insertion point at the beginning of the third calculated field name and type **Max**.

Add Totals and Functions

6. Choose **Design** ›**Show/Hide**→**Totals** Σ on the Ribbon to display the Total row in the query grid.

7. Follow these steps to choose functions for each of the calculated field columns:

(A) Click the **Total** row for the first StayLength column in the query grid and choose **Min** from the drop-down list.

(B) Press Tab to move to the Total row for the next column and choose **Avg** from the drop-down list.

Field:	MinStayLength: Date(	AvgStayLength: Date(	MaxStayLength: Date(
Table:			
Total:	Min	Avg	Group By
Sort:			Group By
Show:	☑	☑	Sum
Criteria:			Avg
or:			Min
			Max
			Count

(C) **Press** Tab to move to the Total row for the next column and choose **Max** from the drop-down list.

8. Choose **Design→Results→Run** 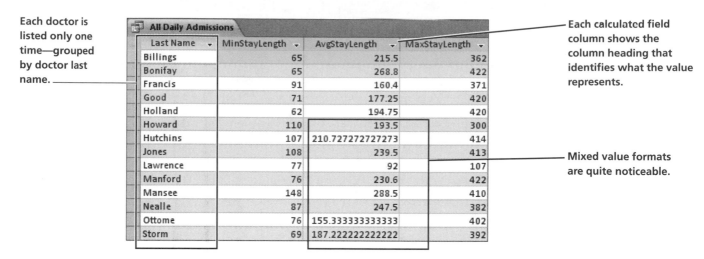 on the Ribbon to display query results and **adjust** the datasheet column widths to display all data and field names.
Your datasheet should resemble the one shown here:

Each doctor is listed only one time—grouped by doctor last name.

Each calculated field column shows the column heading that identifies what the value represents.

Last Name	MinStayLength	AvgStayLength	MaxStayLength
Billings	65	215.5	362
Bonifay	65	268.8	422
Francis	91	160.4	371
Good	71	177.25	420
Holland	62	194.75	420
Howard	110	193.5	300
Hutchins	107	210.727272727273	414
Jones	108	239.5	413
Lawrence	77	92	107
Manford	76	230.6	422
Mansee	148	288.5	410
Nealle	87	247.5	382
Ottome	76	155.333333333333	402
Storm	69	187.222222222222	392

Mixed value formats are quite noticeable.

The number of days you see will differ from those seen here based on the current date on which you run this query.

Format Properties

9. Choose **Home→Views→View** on the Ribbon to switch to Query Design View.

10. Click the **AvgStayLength** field and choose **Design→Show/Hide→Property Sheet** on the Ribbon to open the property sheet and then follow these steps to format the AvgStayLength to display only two decimal points:

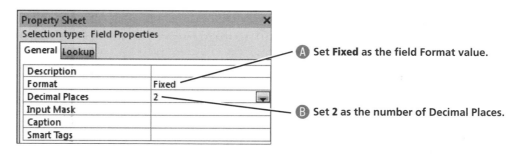

Ⓐ Set **Fixed** as the field Format value.

Ⓑ Set **2** as the number of Decimal Places.

11. **Run** the query again, then **save** and **close** the query.

4.5 Creating Special Types of Queries

Video Lesson   labyrinthelab.com/videos

The queries you have created so far are select queries—queries in which Access selects records according to the fields you add to the query grid and the criteria you set. Access also contains tools for creating a number of special types of queries. In this lesson, you will explore three of these special queries:

■ Crosstab query

■ Find Unmatched query

■ Find Duplicates query

Creating a Crosstab Query

Crosstab queries present data by rearranging the layout of fields in the query results datasheet and grouping the data to summarize it. By grouping fields on the left side of the datasheet and arranging other fields across the top, you can calculate sums, averages, counts, or other totals by group and subgroup. Many users find that using crosstab queries makes it easier to analyze data. For example, if you have a database that contains sales records for insurance agents, the category of insurance they sell, and their total sales for each type of insurance, you could create a crosstab query to display the total sales by category for each agent. Such a grouping and summarization might appear as shown in the following illustrations.

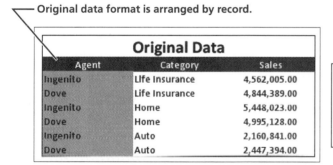

Original data format is arranged by record.

Original Data

Agent	Category	Sales
Ingenito	Life Insurance	4,562,005.00
Dove	Life Insurance	4,844,389.00
Ingenito	Home	5,448,023.00
Dove	Home	4,995,128.00
Ingenito	Auto	2,160,841.00
Dove	Auto	2,447,394.00

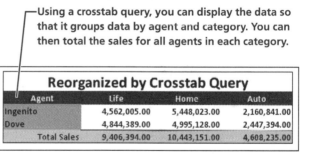

Using a crosstab query, you can display the data so that it groups data by agent and category. You can then total the sales for all agents in each category.

Reorganized by Crosstab Query

Agent	Life	Home	Auto
Ingenito	4,562,005.00	5,448,023.00	2,160,841.00
Dove	4,844,389.00	4,995,128.00	2,447,394.00
Total Sales	9,406,394.00	10,443,151.00	4,608,235.00

Using the Crosstab Query Wizard

As you work with crosstab queries, you will discover a vast difference between the query grid you have used to create select queries and the crosstab query palette. You can, of course, use the palette to manually construct a crosstab query. Until you become better acquainted with the queries, using the Crosstab Query Wizard is most helpful. Crosstab queries can use both tables and queries as the basis of the query.

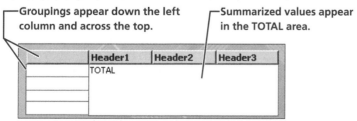

Groupings appear down the left column and across the top.

Summarized values appear in the TOTAL area.

	Header1	Header2	Header3
	TOTAL		

The crosstab query palette organizes data so that it is easier to summarize.

DEVELOP YOUR SKILLS 4.5.1

Create a Crosstab Query

In this exercise, you will create a copy of an existing query, modify it, and use the new query to create a crosstab query that lists each doctor and the total number of admissions for each doctor by department.

Before You Begin: The Raritan Clinic East Queries database should be open.

1. **Right-click** the Daily Admissions query and choose Copy; then **right-click** the query again and choose **Paste**.

2. Type **All Daily Admissions** as the new query name and click **OK**.

3. **Display** the new query in Design view and add the **Department** field from the Doctors field list to the query design.

4. Save changes to the query and then close it.

5. Choose **Create→Queries→Query Wizard** 🖳 on the Ribbon to open the New Query dialog box.

6. **Double-click** the Crosstab Query Wizard to launch the Crosstab Query Wizard and follow these steps to select the query to use for the crosstab query:

A Select the **Queries** option button to display a list of queries.

B Select the **Query: All Daily Admissions** query.

C Click **Next** to display the next wizard screen.

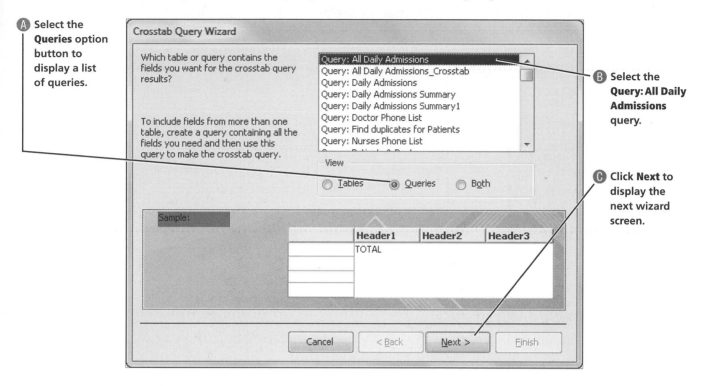

In the second wizard screen, Access wants to know what data you want to display down the left side of the query. In this query, you want the doctor last names to appear down the left column.

7. Choose the **DrLastName** field in the Available Fields list and **move** > the field to the Selected Fields list.

8. Choose **Next**, and then **double-click** the Department field as the field to appear in the column headings.

9. Select **PLastName** in the Fields list and Count in the Functions list to identify the field that contains values and the function you want to calculate.
Your crosstab query grid should resemble the following illustration.

DrLastName field position

Department field position

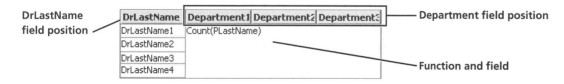

Function and field

10. Click **Next** to display the final page of the Crosstab Query Wizard, and then click **Finish** to accept the defaults Access assigns.

Access runs the query and displays the query results. Your datasheet should resemble the following illustration.

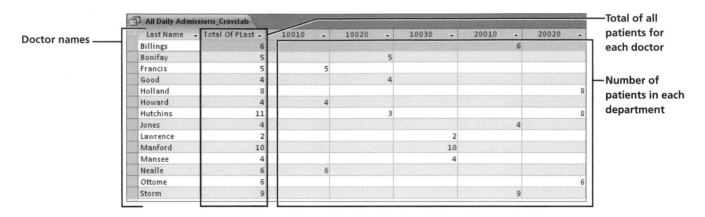

Doctor names

Total of all patients for each doctor

Number of patients in each department

Last Name	Total Of PLast	10010	10020	10030	20010	20020
Billings	6				6	
Bonifay	5		5			
Francis	5	5				
Good	4		4			
Holland	8					8
Howard	4	4				
Hutchins	11		3			8
Jones	4				4	
Lawrence	2			2		
Manford	10			10		
Mansee	4			4		
Nealle	6	6				
Ottome	6					6
Storm	9				9	

11. **Save** 🖫 and **close** ☒ the query.

Naming Special Queries

When you create any of these queries, Access includes the type of query as part of the default query name. You can, of course, modify the query name, but many people choose to include the query type for special queries to make them easier to identify.

Creating Unmatched and Duplicates Queries

Video Lesson   labyrinthelab.com/videos

As you should already know, data contained in database tables often shares fields so that you can include data from multiple tables in queries. As a result, it is important that records entered in one table have a matching record in another table. Sometimes, however, you have a table that simply stores data in the database. The data is related to the company and/or the database, but has no official connection to or field in common with other tables in the database.

Access contains two additional query wizards that enable you to create specialized queries for comparing such data—the Find Unmatched Query Wizard and the Find Duplicates Query Wizard.

- **Unmatched Query**—Locates records in one table that have no related records in another table. For example, you could create an Unmatched Query to ensure that each record in an *Orders* table has a corresponding record in the *Customers* table.

- **Find Duplicates Query**—Locates records containing duplicate field values in a single table or query. For example, you could create a Duplicates Query to locate records in the *Orders* table that were entered twice or to determine the number of a specific item that has been ordered using the *Orders* table.

Identifying the Goal of Unmatched and Duplicates Queries

Reasons for using the unmatched and duplicates queries will vary depending on your needs. Sometimes the goal of each query generated using the Find Unmatched Query Wizard and the Find Duplicates Query Wizard will be to identify no records. Other times, the goal will be to total multiple entries or identify values in one table that have no matching records in the other table. The queries they generate are simply used to compare entries in database tables. Creating and running these types of queries helps maintain the integrity of the database.

Create Unmatched and Duplicates Queries

In this exercise, you will use your Raritan Clinic East Queries database to create an unmatched query to locate doctors in the Patients table that have no matching doctor record in the Doctors table. You will then create a duplicates query to identify duplicate patients in the Patients table.

Before You Begin: The Raritan Clinic East Queries database should be open.

1. Choose **Create→Queries→Query Wizard** on the Ribbon and double-click Find Unmatched Query Wizard.
   Access presents the first screen in the Find Unmatched Query Wizard. From this screen, you select the table you want to check against another table.

2. **Double-click** Table: Patients to identify the table and automatically advance to the next screen.

3. **Double-click** Table: Doctors to identify the table to compare to the Patients table entries and automatically advance to the next screen.
   The next screen (3) displays a list of fields in both selected tables. From the lists, you will identify the field in the Patients table that must have a matching record in the Doctors table.

4. Follow these steps to identify the fields that should match:

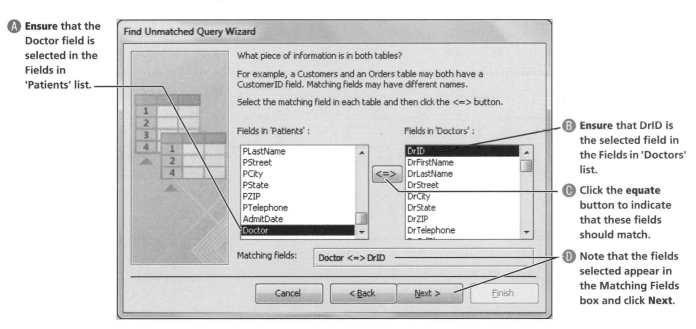

Ⓐ **Ensure** that the Doctor field is selected in the Fields in 'Patients' list.

Ⓑ **Ensure** that DrID is the selected field in the Fields in 'Doctors' list.

Ⓒ **Click the equate** button to indicate that these fields should match.

Ⓓ Note that the fields selected appear in the Matching Fields box and click **Next**.

Screen 4 asks you to identify the field(s) you want to view in the query results.

5. **Move** > the following fields to the Selected Fields list: PLastName, Doctor.

6. Click **Next**, and then click **Finish** to accept the default query name Access assigns.
   The query results datasheet should show no records, the goal of the query. These results ensure that you have a record in the Doctors table for every doctor identified for patients.

Create Duplicates Query

7. **Close** the query, then choose **Create→Queries→Query Wizard** ▦ on the Ribbon again.

8. **Double-click** the Find Duplicates Query Wizard.

9. **Double-click** Table: Patients as the table you want to check for duplicates and to automatically advance to the next screen.

10. **Move** ⟨ > ⟩ the following fields from the Available Fields list to the Selected Fields list, and then click Next: PatientNumber, PLastName, AdmitDate.
   Access now wants to know what additional fields to display in the query results.

11. Click **Next** without moving any additional fields to the Additional Query Fields list, and then click **Finish**.
   The query results datasheet again shows no entries—the goal of the query.

12. **Close** the query and the database, and then **exit** Access.

Viewing Structured Query Language (SQL)

Video Lesson labyrinthelab.com/videos

When you build queries in Access, Access creates the code that contains instructions for displaying the fields and records the query requests according to the criteria you set. In early database programs, those who designed and built the database had to construct the code for displaying the query results. Because Access now does the work for you, it is sometimes interesting to view the code that Access creates for the queries you design. Identifying the instructions Access creates in the code would, possibly, also help you identify reasons why a query might display inaccurate or unexpected results.

In Access, viewing the code is as simple as changing the query view to SQL View. By opening or running a query and changing the view to SQL View, Access reveals the SQL code required to run the query. Study the following illustration of the SQL View for the Find Duplicates query you created in the last exercise.

The first line identifies the tables and fields from the table that are used in the query. It is preceded by the word *SELECT*.

The last part of the SELECT line identifies what action is to occur—in this case, counting patients.

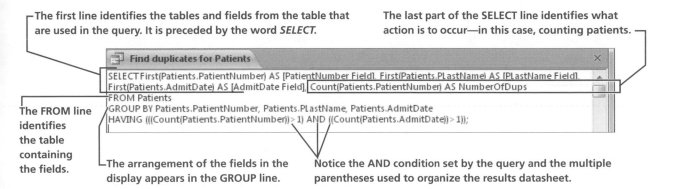

Find duplicates for Patients

SELECT First(Patients.PatientNumber) AS [PatientNumber Field], First(Patients.PLastName) AS [PLastName Field], First(Patients.AdmitDate) AS [AdmitDate Field], Count(Patients.PatientNumber) AS NumberOfDups
FROM Patients
GROUP BY Patients.PatientNumber, Patients.PLastName, Patients.AdmitDate
HAVING (((Count(Patients.PatientNumber))>1) AND ((Count(Patients.AdmitDate))>1));

The FROM line identifies the table containing the fields.

The arrangement of the fields in the display appears in the GROUP line.

Notice the AND condition set by the query and the multiple parentheses used to organize the results datasheet.

4.6 Concepts Review

Concepts Review labyrinthelab.com/acc10

To check your knowledge of the key concepts introduced in this lesson, complete the Concepts Review quiz by going to the URL listed above. If your classroom is using Labyrinth eLab, you may complete the Concepts Review quiz from within your eLab course.

Reinforce Your Skills

Create a Query

The First Perk database now contains several tables—the Coffee Types, First Perk Workers and the Menu Items. In this exercise, you will add a query to the database using the First Perk Workers table so that you have a quick reference telephone list of the workers.

1. Launch **Access**, **open** rs-First Perk from the Lesson 04 folder, and **save** it as a new database named **rs-First Perk Queries**.

2. Select the **First Perk Workers** table and choose **Create→Queries→Query Wizard** to create a query for the table.

3. Select **Simple Query Wizard** and click **OK**.

4. **Move** the FirstName, LastName, and Telephone fields from the Available Fields list to the Selected Fields list.

5. Choose **Next** and then choose **Finish** to accept the default query name and to open the query.

6. **Print** a copy of the query results datasheet.

7. **Close** the query; leave the database open for the next exercise..

Create Queries in Design View

Your database is building nicely. In this exercise, you will create a query based on data contained in the Coffee Types table.

Before You Begin: The rs-First Perk Queries database should be open.

1. Select the **Coffee Types** table, and then choose **Create→Queries→Query Design** on the Ribbon.

2. **Double-click** the Coffee Types table in the Show Table dialog box to add the table to the query grid.

3. **Close** the Show Table dialog box.

4. Starting with the Category Number field in the Coffee Types field list, **double-click** each field name (except the Description field) to add it to the query in the order shown. *When all fields are added, the query grid should match the following illustration.*

Field:	Category Number	Coffee Name	Category Type	Strength	Country of Origin
Table:	Coffee Types	Coffee Types	Coffee Types	Coffee Types	Coffee Types
Sort:					
Show:	☑	☑	☑	☑	☑
Criteria:					
or:					

5. **Run** ! the query and review the results.
Your query results datasheet should appear similar to the following illustration.

Select Coffee Type				
Category Num ↑	Coffee Name	Category Type	Strength	Country of Origin
CECA14	Espresso Roast	Caffeinated	Espresso	Columbia
CFCA22	Holiday Blend	Caffeinated	Flavored	Columbia
CFKA24	First Perk Christmas Blend	Caffeinated	Flavored	Kenya
CLCA	FirstLight Blend	Caffeinated	Light	Columbia
CRAA04	Arabian Mocha Sanani	Caffeinated	Regular	Arabia

6. **Save** 💾 the query using the query name **Select Coffee Type**.

REINFORCE YOUR SKILLS 4.3
Set Query Criteria

One of the tasks users of the First Perk database will have to perform is locating coffee according to different criteria. For example, they may want to locate coffee from a specific country or of a specific type. In this exercise, you will set criteria using the Select Coffee Type query to test it and ensure that it is working properly.

Before You Begin: The rs-First Perk Queries database should be open.

1. Open the **Select Coffee Type** query in your rs-First Perk Queries database.

2. Choose **Home→Views→View** ✓ on the Ribbon to switch to Query Design View.

3. Click the **Criteria** row of the query grid for the Country of Origin column and type **Brazil**.

4. Choose **Design→Results→Run** ! on the Ribbon to run the query.
Access locates only one record in the Coffee Types table.

5. Choose **Home→Views→View** ✓ on the Ribbon to switch to Query Design View.

6. **Double-click** *Brazil* in the Criteria row for Country of Origin and type **Columbia**.

7. Click the **Criteria** row for the Category Type field and type **decaffeinated**.

8. Choose **Design→Results→Run** ! on the Ribbon to run the query.
Access locates three records in the Coffee Types table that meet both criteria.

9. **Close** ✕ the query. Choose **No** when prompted to save changes.
Recall that saving the query with criteria set automatically saves the query with the criteria included.

Create and Format a Calculated Field

Businesses often need to calculate distribution times for sales to ensure that the time between receiving an order and shipping the order falls within their preferred timeframe. In this exercise, you will create a calculated field that is designed to calculate the number of days required to process orders for a company named TechCache and set field properties for the calculated field.

1. **Open** the rs-TechCache database from the Lesson 04 folder and **save** it as new database named **rs-TechCache Queries**.

2. Open the **Customer Order Dates** query in the Navigation Pane, review the data, and then switch to **Design View**.

3. Click the **Field** row of the next available column in the query grid.

4. **Type** the following calculated field exactly as shown:
   ProcessTime: [Shipped Date]-[Order Date]

5. **Drag** the column border to widen the query grid column to you can view the entire entry.

6. **Save** 🖫 changes to the query, and then **Run** ❗ the query.
   Access displays the number of days required to process each order along with other fields in the query results. If your query calculated incorrectly, check the field for typographical errors.

7. Choose **Home→Views→View** 📐 on the Ribbon to return to Query Design View.

Set Calculated Field Properties

8. Select the **calculated field** and choose **Design→Show/Hide→Property Sheet** 📑 on the Ribbon to open the Property Sheet pane on the right side of the query grid.

9. Click the **Caption** property box and type **Days to Process** as the caption.

10. Click the **Input Mask** property box and type **00" Days"**.
    Notice that the space appears after the opening quotations to ensure there is enough space between the number and the word.

11. Choose **Design→Results→Run** ❗ on the Ribbon to run the query again and review the results.

12. **Save** 🖫 changes to the query and **close** ✖ it.

Use Functions in Queries

In this exercise, you will create a query by saving an existing query as a new query. Then you will edit the new query so that it displays the query design you need and use functions to identify minimum, maximum, averages, and counts of records for a query in your sb-TechCache Queries database.

Before You Begin: The rs-TechCache Queries database should be open.

1. **Right-click** the Customer Order Dates query in the Navigation pane and choose **Design View**.

2. Choose **File→Save Object As** to open the Save As dialog box, type **Order Processing Averages** as the new query name, and then click **OK**.

3. Click the **grey column selection bar** for the following fields in the query grid and **press** ⌈Delete⌋ to remove them from the query: Order ID, CustNumber, Order Date, Shipped Date.

4. **Right-click** the grey bar at the top of the ProcessTime calculated field to select the column and then choose **Copy**.

5. **Right-click** the grey bar at the top of the first blank column in the query grid and choose **Paste** to paste the calculated field.

6. **Repeat** the procedure outlined in step 5 to paste the calculated field in the next column.

7. **Double-click** the first instance of ProcessTime and type **MinProcessTime**.

8. **Double-click** ProcessTime in the second ProcessTime column and type **MaxProcessTime**.

9. **Double-click** ProcessTime in the third ProcessTime column and type **AvgProcessTime**.

Add Totals and Functions

10. Choose **Design→Show/Hide→Totals** Σ on the Ribbon to display the Total row in the query grid.

11. Set the function on the Total row for each calculated field to match the **Min, Max, and Avg** function identified by the calculated field name.

12. Choose **Design→Results→Run** ❗ on the Ribbon to display query results.

Format Properties

13. Choose **Home→Views→View** 📝 on the Ribbon to switch to Query Design View.

14. Click the **MinProcessTime** field and choose **Design→Show/Hide→Property Sheet** 📄 on the Ribbon to open the property sheet and then click the fields shown below in the query grid and change the property values to those shown for each field:

Field	Caption	Decimal Places	Format
MinProcessTime	Minimum Process Time	2	Fixed
MaxProcessTime	Maximum Process Time	2	Fixed
AvgProcessTime	Average Process Time	2	Fixed

15. **Run** ❗ the query again, then **save** 💾 and close ✖ the query.

Create a Crosstab Query

In this exercise, you will create a crosstab query that lists each supplier and identifies the number of different items TechCache purchases from each supplier.

Before You Begin: The rs-TechCache Queries database should be open.

1. Choose **Create→Other→Query Wizard** 🖼 on the Ribbon to open the New Query dialog box.

2. **Double-click** the Crosstab Query Wizard to launch the Crosstab Query Wizard.

3. **Double-click** the Table: Inventory item in the first wizard screen to select the table and automatically advance to the next screen.

4. Choose the **Supplier #.Value** field in the Available Fields list and **move** $\boxed{>}$ the field to the Selected Fields list.

5. Choose **Next**, and then **double-click** the Item Type field as the field to appear in the column headings.

6. Select **Inventory Number** in the Fields list and **Count** in the Functions list to identify the field that contains values and the function you want to calculate.

7. Click **Next** to display the final page of the Crosstab Query Wizard, and then click **Finish** to accept the defaults Access assigns.

Edit the Crosstab Query in Query Design View

8. Choose **Home→Views→View** 🖼 on the Ribbon to display the Inventory_Crosstab query in Query Design View.

9. Choose **Design→Query Setup→Show Table** 🖼 on the Ribbon and **double-click** the Suppliers table in the Show Table dialog box to add the table to the query.

10. **Close** the Show Table dialog box.

11. Add the **Supplier#** field in the Suppliers field list to the query grid, placing it in the second column of the grid. where the Item Type field currently appears
Notice that the Item Type, Inventory Number, and Total of Inventory fields move one column to the right to make room for the new field.

12. Click the **Crosstab** row of the query grid for the Supplier # field, click the **drop-down arrow**, and select **Row Heading** from the list.

13. **Run** ❗ the query again, view the display, and then **save** 🖫 and **close** ✖ the query.

Create Unmatched and Duplicates Queries

In this exercise, you will use your rs-TechCache Queries database to create an unmatched query to locate orders in the Orders table that have no matching customer record in the Customers table. You will then create a duplicates query to identify duplicate orders in the Orders table.

Before You Begin: The rs-TechCache Queries database should be open.

1. Choose **Create→Queries→Query Wizard** 🔲 on the Ribbon and **double-click** Find Unmatched Query Wizard.

2. **Double-click** Table: Orders to identify the table and automatically advance to the next screen.

3. **Double-click** Table: Customers to identify the table to compare to the Orders table entries and automatically advance to the next screen.

4. Choose the **CustNumber** in the Fields in the 'Orders' list.

5. Choose the **CustNumber** in the Fields in the 'Customers' list.

6. Click the **equate** button to indicate that these fields should match and click Next.

7. **Move** ▶ the following fields to the Selected Fields list: Order ID, CustNumber, Order Date.

8. Click **Next**, and then click **Finish** to accept the default query name Access assigns.

Create Duplicates Query

9. **Close** ✖ the query, then choose **Create→Queries→Query Wizard** 🔲 on the Ribbon again.

10. **Double-click** the Find Duplicates Query Wizard.

11. **Double-click** Table: Orders as the table you want to check for duplicates and to automatically advance to the next screen.

12. **Move** ▶ the following fields from the Available Fields list to the Selected Fields list, and then click **Next**: Order ID and Order Date.

13. Click **Next** without moving any additional fields to the Additional Query Fields list, and then click Finish.

14. **Close** ✖ the query and the database, and then **exit** Access.

Apply Your Skills

Create Queries Containing Criteria

Cruises provide a wealth of entertainment and adventure for any special vacation. The Cruises table in the as-Keepsake Cruises database contains data that travel agents might use to locate cruises for travelers inquiring about taking a cruise. In this exercise, you will create queries that you will use to locate records for two of the more popular destinations—Hawaii and the Caribbean.

1. **Open** the as-Keepsake Cruises database from the Lesson 04 folder and **save** it as a new database named **as-Keepsake Cruises Queries**.

2. Select the **Cruises** table in the Navigation Pane.

3. **Create** a new query using Query Design View, and add the **Cruises** table to the query grid.

4. **Add** each table field to a separate column in the query design grid and run the query.

5. Switch back to **Design View**, and enter criteria to locate all cruises to **Hawaii**.

6. **Save** 💾 the query using the query name **Hawaiian Cruises** and run the query.

7. **Print** a copy of the query results window and then **close** ☒ it.

8. **Copy** the Hawaiian Cruise query and create a new query named **Caribbean Cruises**.

9. **Edit** the criteria for the Caribbean Cruises query to locate all cruises to the Caribbean.

10. **Save** 💾 changes to the query and **run** it.

11. **Print** a copy of the query results datasheet and then **close** ☒ the query.

Create a Query Using Comparison Criteria

Another common factor in planning a cruise is, of course, cost of the cruise. In this exercise, you will create a query that identifies the sailing dates of cruises that cost less than $1,000. In addition, you will create a second query that identifies cruises sailing during the winter holidays.

Before You Begin: The as-Keepsake Cruises Queries database should be open.

1. **Select** the Cruises table in the Navigation Pane.

2. **Create** a new query in Query Design View and add the Cruises table to the query grid.

3. **Add** all the fields to the query grid except the Ship field and save 🖫 the query using the query name **Affordable Cruises**.

4. **Set** criteria in the query grid to locate all cruises for which an outside cabin costs less than $1,000.

5. **Save** 🖫 changes to the query, **run** the query, and **print** a copy of the query results datasheet.

6. **Copy** the Affordable Cruises query to create a new query named **Holiday Cruises**.

7. **Display** the query in Design View and set the following criteria in the Date field: **Between 12/1/10 and 1/10/11**.

8. **Save** 🖫 changes to the query, **run** it, and **print** a copy of the query results datasheet.

9. **Close** all database objects.

Create a Query

In this exercise, you will create a new query using fields from multiple tables.

1. **Open** the as-First Perk database from the Lesson 04 folder and **save** the database using the name **as-First Perk Queries**.

2. **Create** a new query named **Processed Orders** and add the Orders and Menu items tables to the query.

3. **Add** the following fields from the associated tables to the query grid:

Table	Field
Orders	Items
Menu Items	Price

4. **Run** ⧉ the query and **print** a copy of the query results datasheet.

5. **Save** 🖫 and **close** ⊠ the query.

Create and Format a Calculated Field

The basics for tallying an order using a query are set. In this exercise, you will create a calculated field and format fields in the query. You will continue to use your as-First Perk Queries database in this exercise.

1. Display the **Processed Orders** query in Query Design View and add the **Number** field from the Orders table to the query.

2. Create a **calculated field** in the next available column of the query grid that calculates the total of each item ordered. Use the following values:
   - Field Name: OrderTotal
   - Field from Field Lists: Number, Price
   - Operand: Multiplication (*)

3. **Format** each field in the query grid by setting the following properties for the field:

Field	Caption	Format
Items	Items	
Price	Price	Currency
Number	Quantity	
OrderTotal	Total	Currency

4. **Save** 💾 changes to the query.

5. **Run** ❗ the query and **print** a copy of the query results datasheet.

6. **Close** ✖ the query.

Total Orders Using Functions

Now that the total for each item appears in the query, you can total the value of each order using functions. In this exercise, you will copy a query and save it as a new query, add functions to a query that calculate the total of each order, and use an alias.

Before You Begin: Your as-First Perk Queries database should be open.

1. **Copy** the Processed Orders query and create a new query named **Order Totals**.

2. Display the **Order Totals** query in Query Design view and **remove** the following fields from the query grid: Items, Price, and Number.

3. Add the **Order ID** field from the Orders table to the query grid and position it to the left of the OrderTotal field.

4. **Copy** the OrderTotal calculated field column and **paste** it into the next available column in the query grid.

5. Change the new **OrderTotal** field name to **OT-1**.

6. Display the **Totals** row in the query grid and set the OT-1 column total to Sum.

7. Delete the **OrderTotal** column and then **run** the query.

8. **Print** a copy of the query results datasheet and then **save** and close the query.

Set Criteria in Queries

Each person who orders receives a copy of their order. In this exercise, you will create a new query that is designed to print only the items included on one order. You will continue to use your as-First Perk Queries database in this exercise.

1. **Copy** the Order Totals query and create a new query named **Order 1001**.

2. Display the **Order 1001** query in Query Design View and set criteria in the query that limits the display to only the items for order **1001**.

3. Add the items field to the grid and place it between the other two fields.

4. **Save** changes to the query and then **run** the query.

5. **Print** a copy of the query results datasheet and then **close** the query.

Create a Crosstab Query

Each order placed at First Perk notes the salesperson who served the customer. In this exercise, you will create a crosstab query that displays the total sales for each employee using your as-First Perk Queries database.

1. Display the **Processed Orders** query in Query Design View and add the SalesPerson and Item Name fields to the query grid.

2. **Save** changes to the query and **close** it.

3. Use the Crosstab Query Wizard to **create** a new crosstab query using the Processed Orders query.

4. Choose appropriate settings from Wizard screens to:
   - **Display** the SalesPerson on the left and ItemName across the top.
   - **Sum** the OrderTotal value to calculate total sales by sales person.
   - **Name** the query using the default name Access assigns.

5. **Display** the new query in Query Design View and **format** the properties for each column in the query grid so that it displays appropriately.

The values displayed in the Crosstab Query represent sales and money values. Captions and column Format properties can be set to display the values and identify the columns.

6. **Save** changes to the query, **run** it, and **print** a copy of the results.

7. **Close** the query.

Create Duplicate and Unmatched Queries

Checking the database now that you have created queries using the database tables is important. In this exercise, you will check the integrity of the data using the Find Duplicates and Find Unmatched Query Wizards for your as-First Perk Queries database.

1. **Close** all database objects that might still be open, and then **run** the Find Duplicates Query Wizard to check the First Perk Workers table for duplicate entries and **display** just the employee number, first name, and last name in the results.

2. **Run** ❗ the query and **print** a copy of the query results.

3. Run the **Find Unmatched Query Wizard to** create the following two unmatched queries, **printing** a copy of the query results as you run each query:

   ■ **Compare** the Category # field in the Categories table to the CategoryNumber field in the Menu Items table and display the Description field in the results.

   ■ **Compare** the Orders.Items.Value field in the Processed Orders query to the Item Number field in the Menu Iterms table and display the OrdersNumber field in the results.

4. **Close** ☒ all open database objects, **close** ☒ the database, and **exit** Access.

Critical Thinking & Work-Readiness Skills

In the course of working through the following Microsoft Office-based Critical Thinking exercises, you will also be utilizing various work-readiness skills, some of which are listed next to each exercise. Go to labyrinthelab.com/workreadiness *to learn more about the work-readiness skills.*

4.1 Create Queries

The Raritan database you used in this lesson has additional queries Raritan managers would like to have. Put yourself in the position of an administrator for one clinic department and identify at least four uses for data contained in database tables. Then, determine how this table data could be retrieved using queries. Create two of these queries in the ct-Raritan Clinic East database (Lesson 04 folder), saving the edited database as **ct-RCE Queries**. Run the queries and set properties to improve the appearance of the query results datasheet. Print a copy of the query results datasheets.

WORK-READINESS SKILLS APPLIED

- Serving clients/customers
- Organizing and maintaining information
- Using computers to process information

4.2 Explore Data Online

Raritan Clinic East wants to include a list of local pharmacies in its database so that when patients call in for a prescription renewal, the clinic will be able to quickly locate the phone number to call in the renewal. Go online and locate three pharmacies or drug companies in your area, as well as one mail order prescription service, such as Medco Health. Review their search tools and medications lists. Then, on a clean sheet of paper, develop a list of the fields you would include if you were to build a table for pharmacies. Identify how data from the Pharmacies table might be used to create a query that could be used by all personnel as a quick reference sheet for serving customers when they call for a prescription renewal.

WORK-READINESS SKILLS APPLIED

- Acquiring and evaluating information
- Organizing and maintaining information
- Serving clients/customers

4.3 Get Online Medical Advice

James Elliott has just learned that a number of online services are now offering online medical advice. Such sites enable you to enter a series of symptoms and obtain a preliminary diagnosis that identifies what types of medical issues might cause such symptoms. Locate at least one such site. Explore the site to determine how it works, what sources are used, what search tools are available, and what it costs. If possible, enter a few symptoms (real or imaginary) and see what type of diagnosis it gives. If working in a group, discuss how James might suggest implementing such a service at Raritan Clinic East. If working alone, type your response in a Word document named **ct-Questions** saved to your Lesson 04 folder.

WORK-READINESS SKILLS APPLIED

- Showing responsibility
- Selecting technology
- Improving or designing systems

Index

A

Access, Microsoft
(*see also* databases)
  exiting, 27
  Help feature, 25–26
  importing Excel data, 54–56
  introduction, 7–14
  launching, 7–8
  navigating in, 12–14
  object types, 14
  printing data, 22–25
  window elements, 9–11
aliases in queries, 147
AND criteria in queries, 137, 138
arithmetic operators, 144
Attachment data type, 18, 51
AutoCorrect, 20
AutoNumber data type, 17, 51
Avg function, 148

B

backgrounds
  datasheet row, 76
backing up databases, 61

C

Calculated Field data type, 18, 51
calculated fields, 144–146
caption property, 85, 86, 90
columns and rows
  captions for column headings, 85, 86,
    90
  hiding, 72, 134
  modifying, 72–74, 134
  moving, 72
  sorting, 95–99
comparison operators, 105–106, 134,
  137, 144
copying and moving objects
  in database, 59–61
Count function, 148
criteria, query, 18, 134–141
crosstab queries, 151–154
Currency data type, 17, 51

D

data, defined, 4
databases
  backing up, 61
  closing, 20, 27
  copying, 59–60
  creating from blank, 9–11
  creating objects, 43–56
  Datasheet View, 15–21
  definition, 4–6
  design principles, 34–35
  importing Excel data, 54–56
  navigating in, 12–14, 19
  opening, 35–37
  opening objects, 39–42
  previewing data, 22–25, 108
  printing data, 22–25, 108
  saving, 38–39, 59–61
  security, 35–37
  structures of, 4–5
  table basis for, 5–6
  template-based, 57–59
data dictionary, 34
Datasheet view, 15–21, 72–77
data types
  editing, 79
  function limitations, 147–148
  summary, 17–18, 51
  validation rules, 92
Date/Time data type, 17, 51
dates
  as query criteria, 140–141
  calculating, 145
default value property, 85, 94
descriptions, field, 52
design grid, query, 128–131, 137
Design View
  displaying and using, 50–54
duplicates queries, 152, 154–156

E

Excel, Microsoft
  importing data into Access, 54–56

F

fields
  adding, 78
  aliases in queries, 147
  calculated, 18, 51, 144–146
  default value settings, 85, 94
  deleting, 78, 79
  entering data, 51–52
  formatting, 86–88, 89, 91
  lookup, 18, 51, 81–85
  overview, 15
  primary key, 16, 17, 52, 89, 132
  properties, 52, 85–95, 145–146, 150
  queries, 126, 128–129, 132
  validation rules, 85, 92–94
files, database definition, 15
File table property, 15
filtering records, 103–108
Find and Replace feature, 99–103
Find Duplicates query, 152, 154–156
Find Unmatched query, 152, 154–156
First function, 148
flat file databases, 4
fonts, 76
foreign keys, 16
formatting
  field data, 86–88, 89, 91
  fonts, 76
  forms, 43–45
  input mask property, 85, 86–89, 91
  tables, 72–77
forms
  creating, 43–47
  editing records, 102
  entering data, 45–47
  filtering records, 103–108
  formatting, 43–45
  locating records, 102
  text in, 17, 51
functions
  in queries, 146–150
  types, 147–148

G

gridlines, formatting datasheet, 76

H

Help feature, 25–26
hiding objects
  columns and rows, 72, 134

highlighting
  records for filtering, 104, 105
Hyperlink data type, 18, 51

I

importing data
  Excel, 55–56
input mask property, 85, 86–88, 90, 91

K

keyboard shortcuts
  navigation, 88
  Property Sheet, 145
keys, primary field, 16, 17, 52, 89, 132

L

Last function, 148
layouts
  table, 72–77
logical operators, 134
Lookup & Relationship data type, 18
Lookup Wizard data type, 18, 51, 81–85

M

macros, 35–36
mathematical calculations, order of, 145
Max function, 148
Memo data type, 17, 51
Min function, 148
multiple criteria in query grid, 137,
    138–139
multi-table query, 132, 133

N

Navigation Pane, 12–14
Number data type, 17, 51

O

OLE Object fields, 51
operators
  arithmetic, 144
  comparison, 105–106, 134, 144
  logical, 134
OR criteria in queries, 137, 138
order of operations, 144

P

previewing printouts, 22–25, 108
primary key fields, 16, 17, 52, 89, 132
printing
  data from databases, 22–25, 108
Print Preview feature, 22–25
properties, field, 85–95

Q

queries
  calculations, 144–150
  creating, 124–133
  criteria, 105, 129, 134–141
  crosstab, 151–154
  design grid for, 128–131, 146
  duplicates, 152, 154–156
  fields, 126, 128–129, 132
  hiding columns, 134
  multi-table, 132, 133
  naming, 154
  saving, 135
  select/simple, 124–133
  sorting results, 141–143
  statistical functions, 146–150
  unmatched, 154–156

R

record navigator, 46
records
  adding, 46–47
  database, 15
  deleting, 99–101
  editing, 102
  filtering, 103–108
  finding/replacing, 99–103
  navigating in table, 42
  sorting, 95–99
  updating, 102–103
relational database, defined, 4
reports
  creating, 43, 48–49

S

Save As command, 38, 59
searching, database contents, 99–103
security, database, 35–37
selection methods
  records for filtering, 104, 105
select queries, 124–133
sizing objects
  field lengths, 85, 90
SmartTags, 88
sorting
  data, 95–99
  query results, 141–143
spreadsheets
  importing into Access, 55–56
SQL (structured query language), 156
statistical functions in queries, 146–150
StDev function, 148
structured query language (SQL), 156
Sum function, 148

T

tables
  adding records, 46
  creating, 15–21, 50–54
  deleting records, 99–101
  Design view, 50–56
  from Excel worksheets, 54–56
  filtering, 103–108
  formatting, 72–77
  guidelines, 16
  layout on datasheet, 72–77
  locating records, 99–101
  modifying structures, 78–81
  multi-table query, 132, 133
  navigating records, 42
  organizing data into, 5–6
  saving, 18
  sorting data, 95–99
tabs
  tables, 20
template-based databases, 57–59
text
  field validation rules, 92
  fonts, 76
  forms, 17, 51
  wildcard characters, 106, 136–137,
    138–140
Text data type, 17, 51
Toggle Filter tool, 104
Totals row, 146–147, 149, 161
trusted sites, 36

U

unmatched queries, 152, 154–156

V

validation rules, field, 85, 92–94
Var function, 148

W

wildcard characters, 106, 136–137,
    138–140

Y

Yes/No data type, 18, 51, 79

Z

Zoom feature, 23, 24

Notes

Notes

Notes

Notes

Notes